Discovery at the Rio Camuy

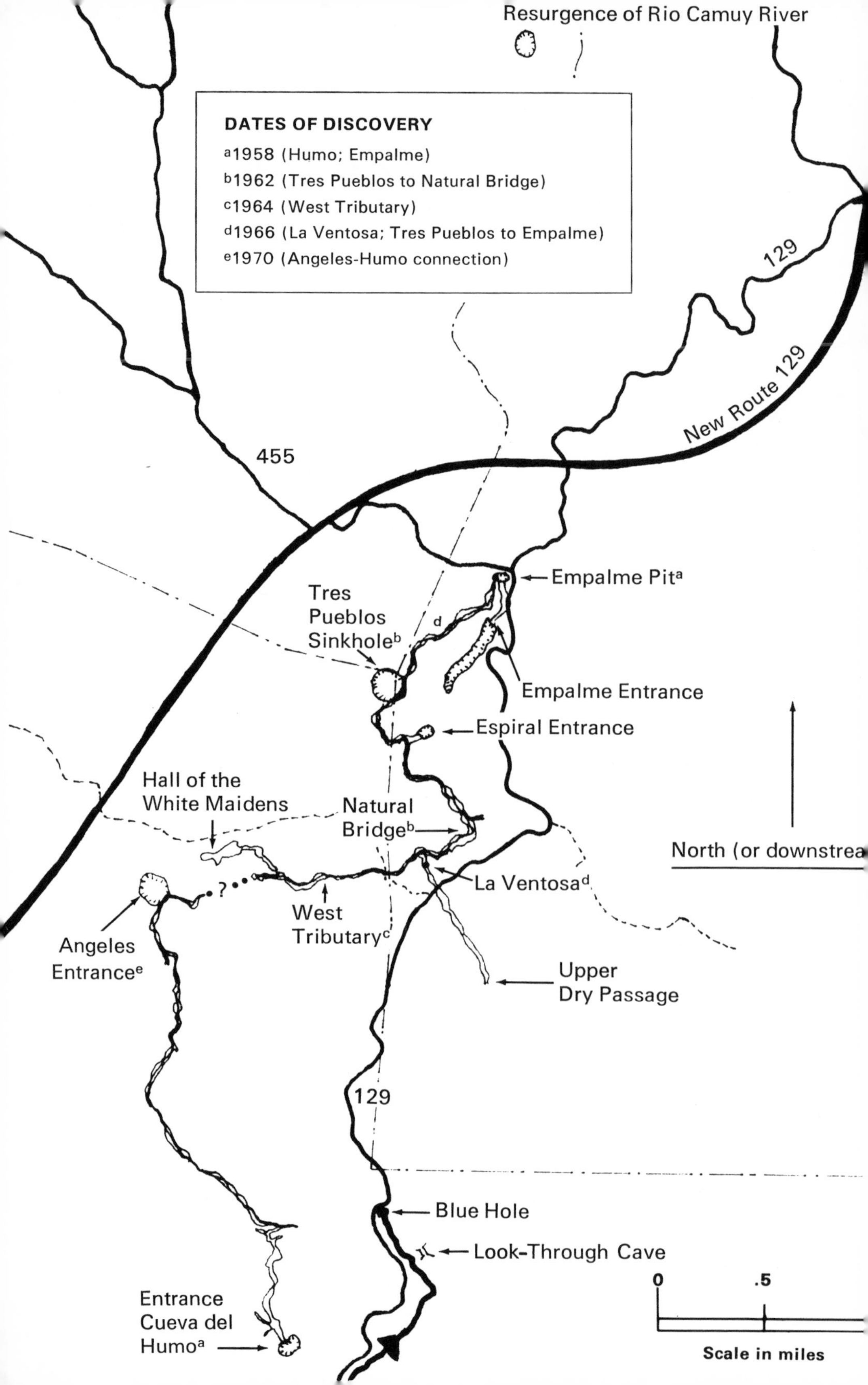
Resurgence of Rio Camuy River
DATES OF DISCOVERY
a1958 (Humo; Empalme)
b1962 (Tres Pueblos to Natural Bridge)
c1964 (West Tributary)
d1966 (La Ventosa; Tres Pueblos to Empalme)
e1970 (Angeles-Humo connection)
129
New Route 129
455
Empalme Pit[a]
Tres Pueblos Sinkhole[b]
d
Empalme Entrance
Espiral Entrance
Hall of the White Maidens
Natural Bridge[b]
North (or downstrea
La Ventosa[d]
?
West Tributary[c]
Angeles Entrance[e]
Upper Dry Passage
129
Blue Hole
Look-Through Cave
0
.5
Scale in miles
Entrance Cueva del Humo[a]

Discovery at the Rio Camuy

BY RUSSELL AND JEANNE GURNEE

Crown Publishers, Inc., New York

Other Books by Russell Gurnee

VISITING AMERICAN CAVES (with Howard Sloane)
CAVE LIFE (with Charles Mohr)

Inquiries should be addressed to Crown Publishers, Inc.,
419 Park Avenue South, New York, N.Y. 10016.

Library of Congress Catalog Card Number: 73-82938
ISBN: 0-517-505940

Printed in the United States of America
Published simultaneously in Canada by General Publishing Company Limited
Designed by Shari de Miskey

For Rafael Limeres, whose enthusiasm and encouragement helped protect Rio Camuy Cave and the land above

ACKNOWLEDGMENTS

Over a hundred lives have in one way or another touched ours in connection with the Rio Camuy and this book. While we cannot list them all, we are particularly grateful to our friends and fellow team members who explored, mapped, photographed, and made scientific contributions above and below ground at the Camuy: David Boyer, Jack Burch, Emily Davis, Edward Zawlocki and the group from Franklin Pierce College, Roy Davis, Gerald Frederick, Jack Herschend, Orion Knox, Joseph Lawrence, José Limeres, Rafael Limeres, Francis McKinney, Forest Miller, Albert C. Mueller, Graham Nelson, A. Y. Owen, Stewart Peck, David and Shirley St. Pierre, Victor Schmidt, John Schoenherr, John Spence, James Storey, Brother Nicholas Sullivan and students from La Salle College, Terry Tarkington, John Thrailkill, Norman Veve, Arlan Wiker, and Alan Zague.

Sincere thanks are also due members of the Puerto Rican administration for their encouragement and work concerning the Camuy, particularly Felix Mejias, Rafael Picó, and Ramon Garcia Santiago.

Through our years of travel to Puerto Rico, our friend Watson Monroe has offered excellent professional help and advice in connection with the geological and topographical aspects of the Camuy area.

We thank our daughter Susan for contributing the account of her brief underground adventure for this book.

And lastly, we would like to thank Herbert Michelman for his fine overall professional guidance.

PREFACE

Every ninety minutes, weather and communication satellites flash overhead gathering data about the earth below. Shutters snap and pictures are sent to a control center on the ground. Is there no place left to explore? What is there for the inquisitive, the imaginative, and the daring to discover? Are we so automated that our heritage to our young people will be the processing of data and the analysis of the output of a mechanical instrument?

The earliest geographical goals on earth have been achieved —the attainment of the Poles and the exploration of the great continents. But there remain opportunities for the individual explorer. The satisfaction and personal thrill of discovery is still possible—under the sea and beneath the earth.

Exploration is like following a piece of twine in a maze. One follows where it leads, surprised at the twists and turns, always eager to see where it originates, but satisfied that the thread is sufficient evidence that one should continue. Often there is disappointment; sometimes there is only a loose end, but occasionally there is surprise and reward.

We have followed such a trail and have achieved some success, but the reward is in the quest and not in the treasure at the end of the journey. The following is a simple story; our thread is the route of an underground river. We have followed it and have exposed a remarkable cave. In this search we have met and worked with many interesting people and have made firm friendships. We have tried to tell the story as it was, without heroics. The cave is the hero here, and we cannot embellish it.

But however huge and impressive, Rio Camuy Cave is extremely fragile. Before Camuy, early in our speleological work, we learned just how fragile caves are, so for the past ten years we have worked to protect the Rio Camuy, above and below ground, as a natural heritage. How well we succeed will be revealed in the next ten years when the new highway near the cave is complete and population pressures push toward the rural areas of Puerto Rico.

Nevertheless, the study of the Rio Camuy Cave will go on for years—for as long as there are passageways or holes to explore, just as there will be many years of original discovery available to anyone who is inquisitive, assertive, and willing to search. Though we chose to become involved with a cave, it could just as well have been a mountain, a lake, or a desert. They are all important to the total environment and to man's relationship to all living things. We hope that as you read this book you will be inspired to find your own Rio Camuy.

RUSSELL AND JEANNE GURNEE

Introduction

It is always easy to look back and isolate an occurrence that was the starting point for a singular adventure, the beginning of a now-completed story, or even a new way of life. It is not always so easy, as we move along in life from one situation to another, to recognize these pivotal occurrences. It is almost impossible to know which incidents will have importance and which will be trivia along the path. However, time usually makes crystal clear those incidents that have affected us personally; and while as individuals we recognize them (through hindsight) they sometimes still remain trivia to the rest of the world.

The incident that pointed my destiny toward Puerto Rico was so commonplace that I didn't realize its significance until years later. It was a snowstorm.

January 14, 1958, in New York City was clear and cold. The weather bureau had predicted snow for upper New York State but a clear day in the city. I called the New York State Thruway offices regarding the road conditions and they informed me that the highway was clear to Rochester—no delays.

I had planned a trip to one of the largest "wild" caves in New York State—Gage Caverns in Schoharie—for the purpose of taking air and water samples in cold weather. I had been in correspondence with George Moore, a graduate student at Yale, about a study he was doing of the carbon dioxide content of drip water in caves. George had summer samples of the drip water in Gage Caverns and now he wanted a sample during the winter. Our plans had been made several months before, and I had asked three other people to go along. I didn't want to change plans, but I was concerned with the weather. The favorable report from the Thruway office eased my mind.

José Limeres, a medical doctor originally from Puerto Rico, and Bob Reville and Charlie Kascur—veteran cavers from the New York City area—arrived at my home in northern New Jersey around 6:00 A.M. and we started on the three-and-one-half-hour drive to Schoharie. We were to meet George Moore and a professor from Yale in Schoharie and then go to the cave.

I had also contacted Jim Gage, the owner of Gage Caverns, and he had said that it was possible to get to the cave without any trouble.

When we arrived in Schoharie, the sun was bright but the ground was covered with twenty-two inches of snow. Huge white tongues of snow covered a lengthy narrow corridor with a deep blanket, leaving only a light covering on either side. This is the "snow belt" that sometimes extends across New York State as a long, narrow plume. Recent storms had dumped this deep cover on the little town of Schoharie, leaving the town of Middleburg (only three miles away) relatively free of snow.

Jim Gage had prepared for our visit by borrowing his friend's army surplus open four-wheel drive command car. It was fitted with snow chains on each wheel and had as a driver an assured and capable fellow who was a stock-car racer on Saturday nights. We all started in our own cars to the nearest road access to the cave.

The road had been cleared, leaving a high ridge of snow along the shoulders, with space between ridge and road wide enough for us to park our cars.

George Moore introduced the Yale professor Dr. Iwatsu, who would be taking the air samples in the cave. He had a huge, covered glass jar for the purpose, about the size of a bell jar. The air from the jar had been evacuated, and he intended to open it in the cave and suck in a sample of the air. This was only part of the equipment we were to take into the cave. Dr. Iwatsu was wearing brown tweed knickers with high knee socks and low shoes. But his equipment nearly covered him as he settled down in the back seat of the command car.

Now seven of us were crowded into the command car as

the driver jockeyed into position—facing the four-foot-high shoulder of snow—and at a running start headed into the apparently solid snow wall. We all expected a crash but the light, powdery snow simply swirled away as we plowed into an open field. The tops of fence posts and telephone poles marked the invisible road to the cave, and the car churned along at a steady pace. The snow surged over the hood but was deflected by the nearly right-angled windshield. And the windshield wipers had no difficulty staying ahead of the swirling snow.

It was about twenty degrees above zero, and a bright, sparkling day. The brisk wind caused by the movement of the car and the excitement of the pulsating, bucking, open vehicle sent a thrill through all of us—the veneer of age and reason seemed to fall away. We were like a bunch of kids on a lark, and it was fun.

The road wound through the woods over level country for nearly a mile. The route passed several fences and continued through several gates. Fortunately the gates were open, as the cattle were all sensibly in the barn.

Several times we had to get out and push when the wheels bogged down in the deep snow or when the car wandered off the road. We were more than enough, so we left Dr. Iwatsu in the rear seat with the jar on his lap and a scarf tied from head to chin.

In a little more than half an hour we reached the clump of trees that surrounded the cave entrance. We shouted encouragement and directions to Dan, the driver, as he drove back and forth to clear an area large enough to turn the car around so that it would be facing away from the cave.

We were in the shelter of the woods, which blotted out the sun, and everyone in the group began to feel the cold. Several of the party beat a trail about a hundred feet long through the snow to the entrance and rigged a safety line to a tree. The entrance to Gage Caverns was an open pit approximately forty-five feet deep, negotiated by a stout ladder of double 2 x 4 sides and ¾ inch galvanized pipe rungs. The top of the pit funneled down twelve feet to about a six-foot opening that was partially covered with a rough wood platform. The ladder projected nearly three feet above the platform. In its entirety, the pit was one vicious-looking slide into the black below.

"Get an ax from the car," I called to the stragglers starting toward the cave. "We'll have to cut steps in the ice to reach the ladder."

In a few moments the first man, secured by a belay, or safety rope, stamped and chopped out a trail down to the ladder and then climbed into the pit. A few minutes later a shout from within signaled that he had descended the thirty-three feet below the platform to the bottom; and we began the slow task of lowering on ropes our equipment—including Dr. Iwatsu's jar.

Because of the treacherous footing around the entrance, only a few men could help and the rest stamped around to keep warm—all complaining that they should have brought heavier clothes.

Finally, six were down in the cave—the seventh man rigging a pulley at the top so that he could be belayed from the bottom in case of a slip. He hastened down the ladder to join the others.

There the equipment was sorted out and taken down a passage away from the open pit, safe from falling ice and loose rock. The temperature at the bottom of the pit was forty-nine degrees, and soon everyone shed his jacket to prevent mud and water from soiling it and to make it easier to work.

The steeply sloping entrance room descended to a level gravel floor, with a blank wall ahead and two knee-high passageways leading off to the right and left. All of us had been in this cave many times in summer but never in winter. We were therefore curious as to the amount of water in the left, main passage now that the ground above was frozen.

I crouched down and looked into the right-hand passage.

"George," I said, "You'll have to take your samples in the Rotunda Room; the boat's gone."

This statement caused several heads to pop into the same opening to verify that the "Bonny Boat"—a square-prowed punt built by Jim Gage inside this tiny passage to permit exploration of the upstream end of the cave—was indeed missing.

"It must have drifted around the bend. Or sunk," I continued.

Checking the other passageway, George decided that the dry portion of the cave would indeed be a better area for his work, so he crawled off to the left, followed by Dr. Iwatsu and his cumbersome jar. The others followed, leaving me with José Limeres and Bob Reville to consider the minor mystery of the "Bonny Boat," which, in a way, originated with the discovery of the cave.

Gage Caverns, formerly known as Gebbard's Cave, was discovered in 1831, and it is one of the largest noncommercial caves in New York State. It was reputed to have had many fine formations, but unfortunately these were removed to grace the cabinets of Mr. Gebbard's mineral collection shortly after the cave was found. It was mapped, and certainly well known locally, but the active stream that flowed throughout its length had prevented commercial development.

Early reports of the original exploration of the cave spoke of "gentlemen of Schoharie" who navigated the river in a wooden boat christened the "Bonny Boat." This original craft has long since disappeared; but Jim Gage, upon his purchase of the cave, decided to replace this practical bit of nostalgia for the convenience of the modern, energetic visitor. We still were hopeful that we could use this aid in getting upstream, so I crawled into the right-hand passage in search of the missing boat.

I came to the shore of a lake formed by the backing up of the stream. The stream, which was quite active up ahead, had characteristically seeped under the entrance room and reappeared farther down the left passage, where George and the others had gone. Where I now stood was the old launching spot for the "Bonny Boat," but no evidence of it could be seen even though we all three concentrated our lights up the passageway.

"How deep is the water?" asked José.

"Only a few feet," said Bob confidently; but when he saw our questioning glances, he ducked back into the entrance passage and returned with a thin pole about four feet long, which apparently had washed in from the entrance.

He took the pole and, leaning out as far as he could, plunged it into the water—up to his wrist. He then tried again, closer to shore, where the stick probed into the mud.

"You see, only a few feet," he said.

We ignored his humor and began to ponder the possibility of retrieving the boat, which we suspected must be just around the bend in the lake. It seemed challenging. Even though we all knew the cave well and there was no mystery in the passage ahead, the lure of exploration—the touchstone of the spelunker—asserted itself; and we all were curious as to whether the boat was "just around the bend."

José was the first to put our common thoughts into action as he put his back against the right wall and started to inch his way along the slippery mudbank. His feet were at right angles to the water's edge and his back was glued to the wall. His fingers searched behind him for holds that would prevent him from falling forward into the water. Fifteen or sixteen feet along the wall, he stopped. The arch of the wall became more acute at the top and he was forced to bend with it toward the water.

"There are no more handholds," he said, and he inched back to where we were standing.

"You almost had it," I said. "There's a ledge that would take you all the way to the bend. It's just a few feet farther along."

"But there's nothing to hold on to."

"Maybe if you could brace your hands on the ceiling. Holding yourself stiff you could get around that tough area."

I realized as soon as I said it that it was my turn to demonstrate what I was suggesting, so I started along the route that José had just traveled until I came to the spot where he had turned back. I was unable to see ahead, but I had seen the ledge before I started so I put one hand in a crevice in the ceiling, leaned over the water, and started the traverse around the obstruction on the wall. One hand, then the next, one step, then another; I was now almost at a forty-five-degree angle but I was past the difficult part and I could see the wide but steeply sloped bank stretching ahead.

As I pushed hard with my arms to come back to an upright position, my feet slipped out from under me and I fell into water up to my waist. The forty-five-degree water took my breath away and I quickly turned and scrambled up the bank. Then I realized that it was too late and that I was already soaked, so I splashed on ahead around the bend and, in an anticlimactic lunge, flopped into the Bonny Boat.

The boat was surprisingly dry—certainly dryer than I was.

I started paddling back the way I had come, hoping that the success of the trip would somehow offset the jeers I expected.

José and Bob were quiet and I wondered why. As I kneeled in the boat and paddled back, steam was rising off my wet clothes causing a fog, which partially enveloped me.

José, the doctor, was the first to speak.

"Russ, you'd better get out of those wet clothes. Remember how cold it is outside."

That was the trouble. The small challenge of the cave, minor as it might have been, had made me forget the return trip, and the snow in the world above. This casual mishap, which normally would only excite laughter and chiding, suddenly took on some importance.

We beached the boat but decided to avoid any further contact with the water. We decided to continue on through the entrance room into the dry passage, where the others had gone. In the broader section of the dry passage I sat down, drained out my boots, and then took off my socks and coveralls. José and I twisted the suit until it knotted, and a stream of water splattered on the clay floor. When no more would drip, I took the suit and flailed it against the flat walls to try to drive out any remaining water. Bob did the same with my socks and, with my teeth beginning to chatter, I put on the soggy clothes again. José had gotten my jacket from the entrance room, and in a few minutes I began to feel better. I continued to stamp around the room while Bob and José went off to find the rest and see how long the collecting would take.

The day passed, and I was feeling pretty good by the time the group returned. But I was embarrassed at my thoughtless action, and quickly launched into a discussion of their work.

After seven hours, at about five thirty, preparations were made to leave the cave; soon after, each explorer slowly climbed up the forty-five-foot ladder and made his way to the command car. I was the last up, and by the time I got to the surface and had pulled up the safety rope, my pants had frozen. They cracked when I walked. The old command car started up immediately and we piled in, this time grateful to be huddled together for the warmth provided.

The sun had gone down and the temperature had suddenly

dropped to ten below zero. There was a bitter, forty-mile wind blowing, and it whipped the powdery snow into swirling, blinding gusts.

In the shelter of the woods, the incoming tracks of our car were plainly visible, and we charged back along through the ruts made only hours before. Beyond the woods and the protection of the trees, it was a different story. The wind had drifted the snow over our old tracks and a new trail had to be plowed, causing the snow to cover the headlights and making the route even more difficult.

There was no shelter between the woods and the road and we were getting farther and farther from the protection of the cave. The trail and driving conditions were getting much worse. We passed the half-mile point from the cave entrance and we were breathing more easily as we bucked and tossed across the next-to-the-last field. Suddenly, about a thousand feet from where our cars awaited us on the road, our right rear wheel threw a chain and we bogged down. Each of us surveyed the damage and no one even suggested attempting to repair it. We each took some equipment (Professor Iwatsu still with his jar) and started wading through the twenty-two-inch snow toward the road. The road was indistinguishable, but the tops of the fence posts flanking it stood out sharply against the snow in the glare of our flashlights.

Dan and some of us who knew the country went ahead to break trail, and we were soon stretched out across the field in a long line. Each step plunged us into snow above our knees, and after a few steps the energy required caused such rapid breathing that we had to pause to rest to prevent the cold air from searing our lungs.

None of us was dressed for this kind of exposure. The line across the field stretched longer and longer as the cold began to numb us. José was just ahead of me and he turned several times to flash the light back to see if I was close behind. My clothes were frozen and my jacket gave little protection from the driving wind. I bent almost double after each step, trying to concentrate on the task of lifting one foot knee high and then putting it down without losing balance. Every third or fourth step I'd slip and lurch up and forward. At first this was painful, but because of the ensuing numbness I began to lose all feeling and the snow seemed merely soft and fluffy, like wading through an enormous bowl of whipped cream. Each time I fell I'd take a little longer to get up. Fortunately José became aware of this and came back alongside me and talked me into getting up, with an encouraging "it's only a few feet farther." By that time, I didn't give a damn where it was; I was tired and the snow looked very soft, and besides, I wished José wouldn't pull at me like that.

Finally, I believed José. It was only a few feet more.

Twenty minutes later, when I sat on the floor of the local diner and poured slush out of my boots and felt the stab of pain in my frostbitten toes, I asked José, "Are there any caves in Puerto Rico?"

"Oh yes! When I was a boy in San Germán, I used to go to a little cave high up on a hill. There should be many caves on the island."

"That does it," I exclaimed. "I've gone into my last New York cave in the wintertime. Let's go to Puerto Rico!"

chapter I

Puerto Rico in 1958 was just beginning to experience the burgeoning tourist traffic that was assuming first position in dollar income for the island. The inexpensive fares offered by the airlines to make it possible for migrant workers to travel from the island to the mainland and the increase in tourism made San Juan's airport facilities probably the most crowded in the Caribbean. The new propeller planes then in service reduced the travel time from New York to about seven hours. The tax-free flight and the special price of $94 round trip brought this beautiful island within easy reach, physically and financially, for large numbers of people from the New York area.

As the plane banked in its approach to the San Juan airport, the growth and activity of the country were clearly visible. We saw rows of hotels under construction along the beach front and skeletons of still more stretching out toward the airport. Only a few hours before, we had left the snow-covered field in New York and now we were sweeping in to a modern landing strip outlined in a brilliant green border of palm trees, and beyond this was the deep, blue-green, white-capped ocean.

The plane touched down, taxied to the terminal, and shut off its engines. The pleas of the steward to remain seated were ignored, as everyone was standing in the aisle with coats and bundles appearing from everywhere before the plane came to a stop.

Our party consisted of Bob and Dorothy Reville, José Limeres, my wife, Jeannie, and myself. José had long wanted to go caving in Puerto Rico; the chance remark that I had made in the diner in New York State had blossomed, only a month later, into this field trip.

The door of the plane swung open and we stepped into the hot, humid air of the tropics. The steady sea breeze sweeping across the field hurried us into the mouth of one of the interminable corridors always found at airports. As we crowded along, shifting our packages, coats, and cameras from arm to arm, we could see in the green-tinted opening ahead crowds of people squinting at our arriving group in search of friends or relatives. We headed toward this tidal wave of greeters and, since we were not expecting anyone to meet us, unhesitatingly pressed into the group, which melted before us, and we continued on through.

"Pepe!" someone called, and José turned and stepped aside. We did not miss him until he called for us to wait. We stopped and saw José approaching with three people whom he hastened to introduce.

His mother, father, and brother had driven across the island from San Germán that morning to meet him, and the excitement of the meeting was still in the tear-stained eyes of his mother and the smiling face of his father as they vigorously shook hands with all of us. His brother, Jorge, stood shyly by as we all spoke at once. José was the oldest son, a successful doctor, and they had all been anxious to see him.

José's father, a white-haired, energetic man, bubbled with enthusiasm and swept us up with his welcome to the island. We forgot the snow and cold we had just left; we were transported into the blazing sunlight and were warmed by the vitality of the people.

We chatted and ignored the crush of the airport crowd as we retrieved our luggage, rented a car, and prepared for our quest of the caves.

José's father, Rafael Limeres, was a retired schoolteacher and lifelong resident of Puerto Rico. He began telling us of the attractions of his home town, San Germán, "the best little town on the island." It was he who had taken José to his first cave; and this had been the beginning of José's interest.

In the brief time we had to plan this trip, I had attempted to get some information about the island's caves. It came as a surprise to me to find that there was nothing in print directly related to the subject. I found some references to caves in the New York Academy of Science papers on the study of bats on the island, but nothing specific about the cave regions.

Based on a geological map I had obtained, we planned a combination sight-seeing and surveying trip for the brief ten days we had allotted for the task. The map showed that the largest and most interesting area of limestone (the rock in which most caves are found) was in the northwestern part of the island. We therefore decided to make a tour starting in the east, working all the way west across the island (through San Germán) and ending in the vast northwestern limestone belt stretching from Utuado to Arecibo and from Morovis to the Rio Guajataca.

Dorothy and Bob Reville had traveled with us many times in the United States, and we knew their interest and proficiency in caves. Here, on the island, more facets of their varied expertise came to the surface. Dorothy, who had been on the publication staff at the New York Zoological Park for many years, found time to do some bird-watching in a region where so many of the birds were strange and unusual to us. One, the ubiquitous cattle egret, was in nearly every pasture on the island. This bird has followed domestic cattle all over the tropical world. We watched flocks of them, with their quick, alert motions as they followed close behind the cattle, snatching up the insects flushed out by the animals' shuffling feet. Unfortunately many of the small birds and animals of the island have been killed for food and sport by the human population, which has destroyed much of the natural fauna.

Bob, with Con Edison in New York, had a thorough

knowledge of geology and mineralogy, which was invaluable in prospecting for caves. The nights, however, were made more entertaining by Bob's knowledge of astronomy. The crystal clear skies, unsullied by the haze of the large northern cities with their millions of particles of airborne dust, showed more stars than we imagined existed. We spent hours watching the star showers and tracing the highly imaginative descriptions of the constellations as observed by the ancient students of the stars.

The first days passed very quickly. Every turn in the road brought a new and interesting scene. We spent our time leisurely driving over the narrow twisting roads, drinking *cerveza* at the local cafés, and asking the local people about caves.

José was very happy. For quite some time he had been imprisoned by his calls along the drab, snowy streets of Newark, New Jersey—staring down inflamed throats, prescribing cold tablets, setting broken bones, and so on. Now he was released on his sun-drenched homeland. He was a boy again with the opportunity to explore the caves he was unable to visit in his youthful years in San Germán. His enthusiasm was contagious, and we were all enthralled with the possibility of exploration and discovery.

When we came to San Germán, it was also to the celebration of the homecoming of José; we were drawn into the warmth and friendliness of family life so characteristic of the Puerto Rican people.

Later José took us to see the cave that was his first introduction to the sport. He was a little embarrassed by his realization that this little cave was much larger in his memory; when he was a small boy, exploring it had been much more of an adventure. We all understood, as the same thing had happened to us. The schoolhouse that seemed so huge and frightening to Jeannie and me is just a tiny annex to a new school building; through adult eyes, we wonder how we could have ever imagined it was anything special.

There was a treat in store for us in this little cave, however, as we were made conscious of the tremendous amount of life that exists underground in the tropics (in comparison with the cold, sterile caves of the temperate zones). The roots of vines and trees sent down deep into the cave tenuous feelers,

In San Germán, José Limeres climbing a cable ladder (alongside tropical vines). *Russell Gurnee*

sometimes a hundred feet long, in search of moisture. These tendrils resembled elevator cables reaching down into the blackness. Spiderlike creatures, sometimes a foot across, scuttled ahead of us as we probed the darkness with our flashlights and lamps. Land crabs hid in the darkness of the passages, and the clanking of their armor was unnerving to us, accustomed as we were to the tomblike stillness of northern caves.

By the end of our time on the island we had covered almost all the karst, or eroded limestone, regions and sampled all the types of caves to be seen. We had only to visit the northwest corner and then we could say that we had made a complete tour. We had mapped twenty-four caves, and all were dry, dusty, and more or less typical of those in the Caribbean.

We started our return trip northward from San Germán to San Juan through the Lares region without much enthusiasm or expectation of finding anything very unusual, but just north of Lares we entered "haystack" country. Immediately the terrain became startling and interesting. Imagine a region of several

Aerial view of karst hills. *James Storey*

LOCATION MAP OF PUERTO RICO

The Camuy River, originating in the midland plateau of northwest Puerto Rico, drains about 25 square miles of gently sloping Cretaceous rock and flows north to the ocean. In its route to the coast, it sinks underground at a place called "Blue Hole" and for about five miles flows a subterranean course, reappearing in a canyon.

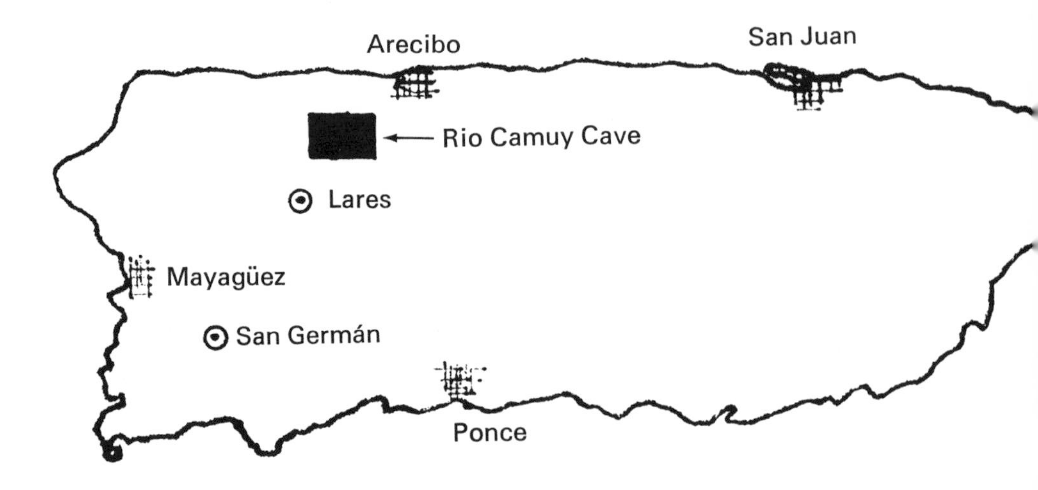

hundred square miles covered with little cone-shaped hills, two to three hundred feet high. Imagine these hills pushed so close together that their bases blend—like thousands of eggs standing on end, half submerged in green foliage. This gives a rough idea of the karst topography in that section of Puerto Rico. The road that traverses this region was cut out of the steep slopes of these hills paralleling the valley of the Rio Camuy. As we climbed higher and higher above the valley, the river, the Camuy, appeared as a tiny twisting snake crawling along the bottom of the canyon below. We stopped the car to take pictures, and José remained to ask one of the little boys who appeared to pop out of nowhere whenever we stopped whether there were any caves around. The boy pointed in several directions, and we knew we had arrived. Although we did not know it at the time, we were within sight of at least a dozen caves and were on top of the entrance to the daddy of them all—Rio Camuy Cave.

José beckoned to us; and, with the little boy acting as guide, we walked back down the road a few hundred yards where we could look across the valley—right through the next mountain! On the opposite side of the river, halfway to the top of one of the haystack hills, was a large black cave opening at least a hundred feet wide and sixty feet high. By aligning ourselves in the proper position, we could see sunlight at the other end of the tunnel as it streamed in on the far side. The upper part of the opening was a silhouette of stalactites hanging in serpentine shapes from the roof of the cave.

While my companions were occupied photographing this attraction, I returned to the car and started to get out my caving gear. The bug of exploration had bitten me badly, and I had to exhibit considerable restraint when the group suggested we eat before investigating the caves.

José now questioned the half-dozen boys who had appeared, and by the time we had finished our sandwiches the plan of action was decided. We would not visit the "look-through" cave, but another, known locally as the Cave of Smoke—*La Cueva del Humo*. This cave, about a half mile away, was described as *muy grande* and much more interesting than the little cave across the river. By this time, the inhabitants of a little house close by had joined our group; and Jeannie and Dorothy were invited to

Look-Through Cave. *Russell Gurnee*

use the house to change into caving clothes, after which we would all hike to the entrance.

We were assured that Humo Cave was large and would require lights; with great enthusiasm we filled our carbide lights and checked our flashlights. Fully equipped, with the boys leading the way, we started up to the top of one of the haystack hills, down the other side, and then along a low ridge. The trail was well traveled and was the only access to the many little houses in the area. In the windows, the curious glances and smiles that greeted us were friendly and inquiring. We continued on, up and down the steep hills. Just as we were about convinced that we had gone at least over a mile—straight up—one of the little boys called back and pointed over the next ridge to tell us we were nearly at the cave. A steep slope led us down to a huge sinkhole. On one side was a broad-arched opening to an inviting-looking cave—Humo. The arch was fringed with long, white stalactites, and the cool breeze from the opening encouraged us to enter.

While we lighted our lamps and put on our hard hats the boys went on ahead. We found them waiting for us on top of a large mound of calcite just within the entrance to the cave. The first room, after our eyes had adjusted to the dim light, appeared to be all there was to the cave. In a minute, however, we realized that behind the boys there was a dark passage leading off to one side. We climbed up and soon left the outside world behind as we walked down a broad, high corridor. The cave was dry and dusty, but it was encouraging to find that the passage pitched steeply down into the mountain. Air blew toward us and we pushed ahead, mapping our way with compass and steel measuring tape as we progressed. We passed through several large rooms, ever descending; and, as the station points grew on our notebooks, we were confident that this was a larger cave than we had seen anywhere else on our trip. This descending passage led into a long, larger one, where we were perched on a shelf overlooking still another room ahead. The boys assured us that there would soon be a river, but we would have to use ropes to get to the bottom.

We decided that this would be a good room to photograph. José was elected to go on ahead and set off flash powder charges to light it while the rest of us stayed at the top and tended the cameras. An aluminum ladder was taken from a pack and a safety line was secured to José. We watched him climb down the twenty feet to the bottom of the boulder-strewn passage.

Entrance to Cueva del Humo. *Edward Zawlocki*

Taking flash pictures in a large room necessitates providing a tremendous amount of light. This problem was solved many years ago by early photographers who used magnesium powder (sometimes called smokeless flash powder). It produced optimum light with minimum equipment. Unfortunately, disadvantages of this method have made it almost obsolete today. The obvious problem is the explosive nature of the powder itself. It is so dangerous that it is unlawful to sell it without a license or to send it through the mails. The second problem is the amount of smoke produced. The British, who still use this method of lighting, call it flashless smoke powder—with just cause. Usually it is possible to get only one exposure—then you must wait for the smoke to clear. In spite of these objections, it still is the best method for lighting a large cave room. One thimbleful of powder provides enough light to photograph a room seven hundred feet long. (It also produces enough heat to give a third-degree burn if you are too close to it.)

José carefully set his charges of powder on waxed paper (to prevent moisture from spoiling the flash), made little wicks of waxed paper to light the charges safely, and called to us that he was ready. All the cameras were on tripods, set on bulb (time exposure). On signal, the lenses were uncovered in anticipation of the flash from below. José lighted one charge. The tiny flicker of the wick stealthily crept toward the powder charge. VROOM! The explosion and concussion rocked the whole cave. The lightning flash briefly lit the huge room in front of us. We had one exposure. We covered the lenses of our cameras while José hurried over to the second charge and repeated the operation. This time the smoke from the flash had reached the ceiling, and suddenly we were in the midst of a circling mass of bats. Hundreds of them were trying to get out of the room, and we were in the only passageway. True to their unerring guidance mechanism, none of them touched us. But for a few minutes we were in the midst of a snowstorm of black flakes. Though it seemed inevitable that we would be struck by these hurtling objects, they always veered around us and, in a few minutes, they were gone.

Meanwhile, José had gone on down to the end of the room to verify that there was a river below, and in a few minutes he was back at the foot of the ladder ready to join us. We decided that it would be best to continue our exploration another time, and packed our gear and headed for the entrance. The survey showed over a half mile of passageway, a most encouraging sign for the caves of this area.

It was late afternoon when we returned to the car, and we had only touched the edge of this vast karst region. We were surrounded by canyons whose walls were covered with exposed stalactites. Several miles farther north along the road we stopped again, partly because of thirst and partly to ask the people about this remarkable cave area. Although we did not know it, the main passage of the underground route of the Rio Camuy was directly below us. This strange and somewhat harsh landscape would become as familiar to some of us, in the years to come, as our own hometowns.

We stood in the entrance of a little store having soft drinks and beer. At one end of the room some local youths were playing pool and casting furtive glances at us. José had entered the store and engaged Señor Perez, the owner, in conversation; and we soon all joined in when we discovered that he had seven children all living in the United States. He himself had lived in Newark for a number of years. When the inevitable question of caves came up, he came out from behind the counter and led us across the road to a thick barrier of trees and brush.

"*Tenga cuidado* (Be careful)," he admonished as he gingerly separated the branches and stood aside so we could peer through the opening. The scene was astonishing. The clearing below the trees seemed to have no bottom. We were standing by the side of the road on the edge of a huge pit more than one hundred feet in diameter and, from our vantage point, bottomless.

"If you listen, you can hear the river," he said. We all stood quietly and could hear faintly deep below us the murmur of rushing water.

"El Rio Camuy."

The brush and vines so thoroughly concealed this pit that we took a dead branch and hammered down some of the foliage so that we could better see the dimensions of the opening. The opposite side was clearly visible and we could see that the opening was undercut—the area below belling out.

"There's nothing below us," said Bob as he lay on the rock

Air view of Empalme pit. The horizontal road is Route 455; the one seen vertically is Route 129. Perez's store is at the junction of 455 and 129. *National Geographic Society*

and looked over the edge. He meant that there was nothing but space between the projecting thin shelf of rock and the black pit below.

We all looked at one another and had the same common thought: We didn't have enough ladder or rope to explore this huge pit. Knowing we didn't have the equipment made the hole all the more interesting and attractive.

"Would you like to see the cave?" our guide interrupted our thoughts. "Of course!" we said, and he grinned at our enthusiasm.

He turned and went back to the store to find one of the young men who were playing pool. "It is very easy," the storekeeper said. "This man will show you." He then introduced us to Sixto Irrazi, a well-built man in his early twenties with black curly hair and a wide smile. Sixto explained that it was possible to get to the bottom of the pit through another entrance that led through a cave not far from the store. He further said that we did not need any special equipment, only flashlights. As it was getting late, we were anxious not to lose any time and urged him to lead on.

We followed a well-beaten path for a few hundred yards, and then we started to descend into a deep ravine. The trail was steep and we slipped and slid, gripping vines and branches as we went until we were deep beneath the trees that covered the bottom of the ravine. At one point the trail turned back toward the road, and then we again descended steeply toward what appeared to be a high, blank wall. The trail was now covered with loose mud and the vegetation was more luxuriant. The trees were dripping with moisture as we became enclosed in a rain-forest environment—the sun being hidden by the thick, damp foliage overhead. The whole world seemed to take on a greenish hue, unreal and ethereal. We continued on through a grove of banana trees growing sturdy and strong in the black topsoil of the floor. Then we saw the object of our hike: the entrance to a cave, with green, moss-covered stalactites festooning its roof. As we followed Sixto along the trail we again descended and in a few minutes were standing within the broad opening of a subwaylike tunnel which stretched ahead into the blackness. The floor was perfectly smooth; the walls were a hundred feet apart; and the ceiling, decorated with stalactites, extended sixty feet over our heads. This was a classic, textbook entrance.

Sixto, to whom all this was familiar, had gone ahead of us, and we hastened to follow. About four hundred feet farther on we caught up with him. We were standing at the elbow of an L-shaped tunnel having approximately equal legs. Behind us was the arch-shaped opening we had entered, and to our left was a similar opening about the same distance away. The only difference between the two was that the second opening was into the side of a pit—the one we had seen from above only half an hour before. The floor was slippery and wet—from the water dripping from the roof—as we picked our way to the left over the puddles and broken rock toward the pit.

We all gathered at that opening and looked up at the blue sky framed by the green-fringed hole. It was like being at the side of an enormous natural jug 400 feet in diameter and 400 feet deep. From above, the opening, only 150 feet, and oval in shape, admitted enough light for us to see the entire area clearly. As we thought, the pit was truly undercut, the green fringe of foliage extending down only as far as the terminal points of

Inside Empalme Cave looking out of the entrance that leads back to the ravine. *National Geographic Society*

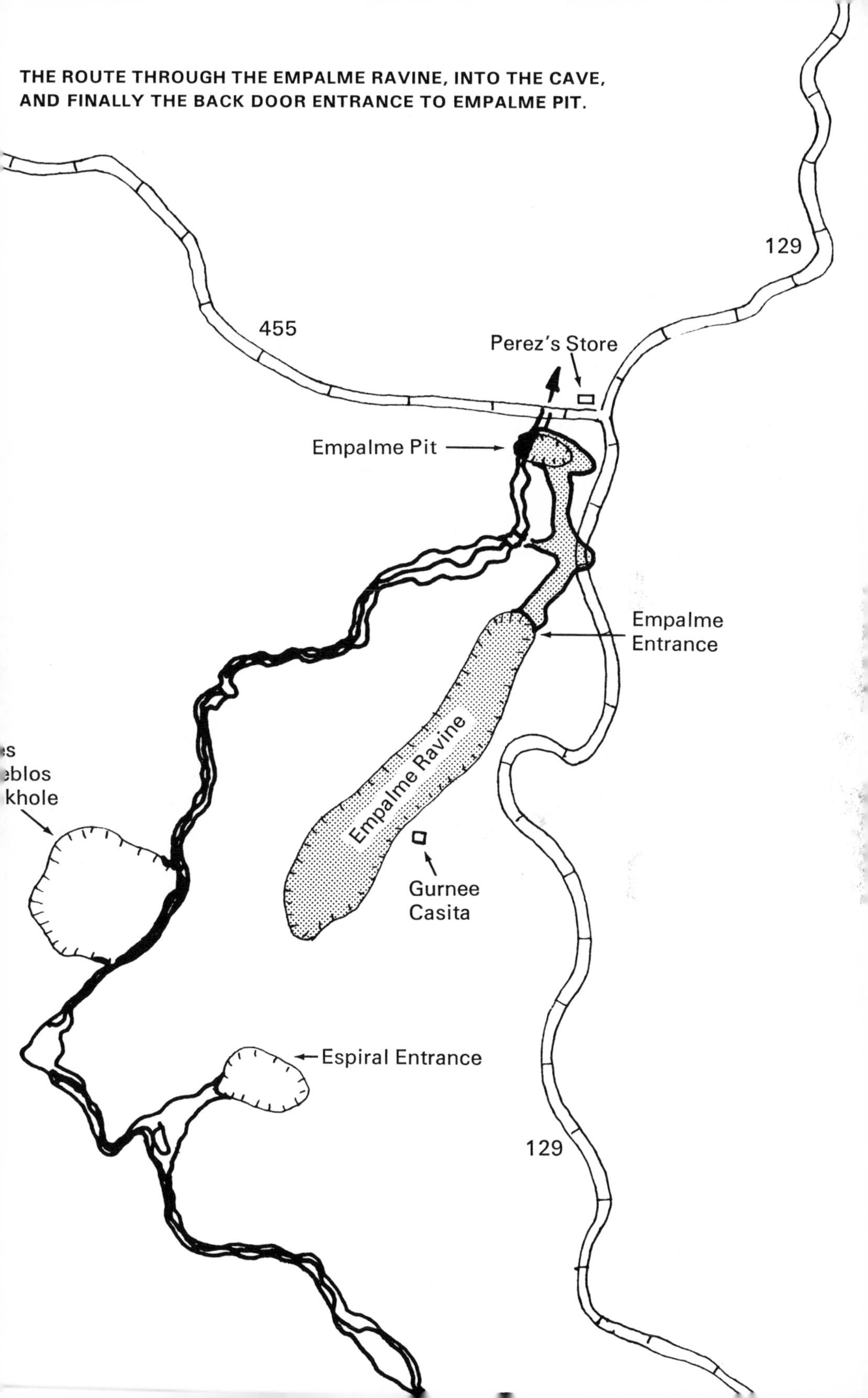

THE ROUTE THROUGH THE EMPALME RAVINE, INTO THE CAVE, AND FINALLY THE BACK DOOR ENTRANCE TO EMPALME PIT.

Interior of Empalme Cave. *José Limeres*

Looking at the sky from the bottom of Empalme pit. *Mills Tandy*

vines. All around were barren rock walls, fragmented by the periodic collapse from weathering. The floor was a chaotic jumble of this loosened rock (scree) and steeply sloped to one side of the pit, where we saw and heard the Rio Camuy, now much larger than the tiny stream that we had seen disappear only a few miles to the south. But it was still coffee-colored and flecked with white foam.

The river could not be ignored. The noise of the rushing water and crashing rapids was amplified by the rocky chamber. The murmur of an hour before was now a roar. It was hard to associate the narrow strip of water we had seen earlier with the sound that seemed to come from everywhere. Sixto pointed down to the river and we gathered around him.

"That is the chassis of a truck that went off the road and ended in the river." There below us we could see the naked frame of metal, less than one third the width of the stream. The chassis was tilted and only a few feet of the bars were out of the water. This gave us some scale for the size of the river, which must have been at least twenty feet wide and six feet deep.

"He died," Sixto said simply as he looked first at the raging waters and then up to the surface of the pit. We could imagine that awful plunge and the crushing impact as the truck bounced and careened down into the river. This sobering thought filled our minds as we picked our way down through the weeds and vegetation growing on the rocky slope to the edge of the water. At the bottom the sound was deafening. The surging water seemed to come from a high, arched opening in the side of the pit, from where it roared across the bottom of the pit and then disappeared into an ugly looking siphon on the far side. It looked so dangerous and treacherous that we hesitated a few feet from the slippery shore. I picked up a stick, tossed it into the river and watched it get swept off into the rapids, bobbing along, until with a sickening slurp it plunged under the wall at the far side.

We turned and climbed back to the tunnel we had come through to see this pit. We had all brought cameras, and so we again got out the flash powder and, after the usual explosions and choking smoke, we packed our cameras, hopeful that we had recorded this remarkable scene.

It had begun to rain and the return trail was rapidly becoming awash, with each branch we touched releasing a shower. And it was almost dark outside. By the time we returned to the road, it was pitch black; the streaming light from doors, windows, and cracks in the walls of the little store looked very inviting.

We were assured by the storekeeper and Sixto that it was possible to wade upstream to a waterfall just inside the arched upstream opening, but no one had explored the river farther. We asked where the Rio Camuy again reappeared, and they both told us that the river continued underground for several more miles, where it surged up out of the ground in the gorge of the Camuy. It then flowed as a surface stream into the ocean on the north coast.

We thanked our host, gave Sixto something for his kindness, and started on our long drive back to San Juan, elated at our last glimpse of the caves in this portion of the island.

The next day we boarded a plane for New York, hoping that we might again return to the island, but not too optimistic about exploring the Rio Camuy. The equipment and manpower necessary for such seemed beyond our resources. We felt that

View from the back door overlooking the river. The remains of the truck chassis can be seen in the lower center. *José Limeres*

we had had just a tantalizing peek at something we couldn't finish.

We returned to our individual occupations: Jeannie and I drew up the maps of the trip, published our reports in the National Speleological Society's *News,* and tendered a report on "The Caves of Puerto Rico" to an international speleological congress we attended several months later in Italy. All of us considered the episode completed and that we were destined to spend our spare time investigating those regions closer to home.

Three years went by and the incidents I have described had become only a pleasant memory. My interest in caves had not flagged, but I had become involved in the administration of the National Speleological Society to the extent that I had been elected president, and so my free time (outside of that devoted to my business) was limited.

Until I received a certain telephone call.

During Christmas week of 1961 one of the senior editors of *Life* phoned me regarding a spelunking story for the magazine. As I was also the public relations officer for the National Speleological Society, I arranged to meet with Marshall Smith of *Life* to discuss possibilities.

Life wished to take candid shots of a local caving trip to a typical spelunkers' cave in preparation for an "adventure" story. The approach was an innovation for *Life,* and they were enthusiastic that spelunking would be of interest to their readers. Unfortunately, I did not agree that this would be to the best interests of speleology. I felt that the publicity created by the article on the local cave would cause a flood of people to visit it. Since we did not own any of the caves we might use, it could prove damaging to owner relations if the cave was publicized without controlled access after the piece was published.

This problem brought the interview to an impasse until I reached back in my memory and suggested that we might have a real adventure story if we were to have a field trip to explore an underground river in Puerto Rico. This compromise was enthusiastically received.

Soon after, I dug out the photos we had taken in Puerto Rico and began to plan for a return to the island. As I reviewed the area we had visited, I became excited over the possibility of returning. The mechanics of the expenses and personnel were agreed upon with *Life* and the date was set for the third week of February, 1962, as this was the end of the dry season—possibly the best time to explore an underground river safely.

Gone was the mere general hope that I would one day explore the Rio Camuy. Now I had the obligation, the responsibility. I had agreed to prepare, undertake, and attempt to make the underground traverse—from the entrance we had seen among the haystack hills of northwestern Puerto Rico to the disappearance of the river four air miles away. I was not sure we would be able to accomplish this, but I felt fairly certain we would be able to provide *Life* with an adventure story well worth photographing.

It was up to me to make the preparations. I realized we would be exploring an unknown and possibly dangerous cave—under the scrutiny of the most powerful of critics, the press of the United States. A photographer from *Life* would cover all our work, and if we were to achieve a successful exploration, we would have to do it without the comfort of a backup rescue team of friends and experienced cavers. Further, to present any kind of representative picture of original exploration, we could not play it safe; we had to enter the unknown. Here was a paradox. How could we provide the required and agreed-upon "adventure" without the risk of putting the National Speleological Society, as well as speleology itself, in a position that might make it seem a reckless, hazardous occupation? All I could do was prepare as thoroughly as possible and use the best available personnel.

Life left us with the complete responsibility for the details of the expedition—with the exception that they chose the photographer (acceptable to us of course). We would be a part of the team and we were to provide the environment for his camera.

On the credit side of the project, we did have experienced men to call upon in planning the venture and to make up the team. In 1954 the National Speleological Society had run an official expedition to explore the innermost portions of Floyd Collins' Crystal Cave in Kentucky. A party of sixty people explored this cave for a week. The story of that trip and the resulting knowledge gained were published in a book, *The Caves Beyond.* I was a member of that team, so naturally I turned to them for help. The leader, and originator, of that expedition was Joseph Lawrence, of Philadelphia, who collaborated with Roger Brucker to write the book.

Another member was Albert C. Mueller, of Cranford, New Jersey. In the years following the trip Al and I had become close friends and had explored many caves together. Al and Joe came to mind when I began my plans, and so we arranged for a meeting.

It was agreed that we must have a minimum of five (six with the photographer) for a safe number. We chose José Limeres to accompanying us; he was indispensable. He knew the language, and was an excellent caver and a medical doctor. This left us with only one berth to fill. We were solid on experience, but we realized that we must have someone particularly proficient in rope work and climbing techniques.

We agreed that we would have to ask for help in the selection of this young, vigorous caver. We put in a call to one of the largest grottos (chapters) of the Society in Pittsburgh and asked them to submit the name of a qualified member. (The Pittsburgh Grotto's caving territory is West Virginia, whose caves most represented the challenge and the problems of the Rio Camuy system.) In a few days we were provided with the name of Jerry Frederick, of Pittsburgh.

Our next problem was equipment. Here we called upon John Spence, another friend and member of the original trip to Floyd Collins' Crystal Cave. John, a retired executive of the Ackerly Camera Company, had, for nearly twenty-five years, outfitted—from shoelaces to elephant howdahs—many expeditions for the American Museum of Natural History, and it was a delight for him to prepare the equipment and material necessary for this trip. We reviewed our experience in water caves, hoping to cover all the possibilities that might arise. The most critical equipment was some type of water transportation. We settled on three navy surplus two-man rubber boats. Then the communication problem was attacked by John, who came up with a two-way telephone with a sound-powered backpack.

We had less than three weeks to prepare; and, though we

were able to line up our team and equipment quickly, we began to worry about the team's unknown sixth member—courtesy of *Life* magazine. The photographer chosen to go on the trip was in Ecuador covering a landslide and was not scheduled to return until a week before our departure. I learned that he had never been in a cave and planned for his return a trip to West Virginia to try out his camera equipment.

The time drew close. We had our plane reservations and all the equipment. But no photographer. The week before we were to leave I received a call from *Life* telling me that the photographer had intestinal flu and that they would substitute another man. I was a bit shaken by this news; and while they gave me the man's name and location, I had visions of our plans being fouled up by this last-minute change.

"He'll call you tonight; you make arrangements directly with him," said the *Life* man.

I murmured my assent and hung up. I thought wildly about the change in plans, the improbability of our arranging for a preliminary trip and the possibility that this man might require briefing that we would not have time to give him.

Eleven o'clock that night I received a call from Oklahoma City. It was the photographer, A. Y. Owen. After he had introduced himself I timidly asked if he had ever been in a cave.

"Oh yes," he said, "Quite a few."

It turned out that A. Y. had been a member of the National Speleological Society for fifteen years and had photographed Neff Canyon Cave on a field trip several years before! This was the deepest known cave in the United States at that time, and he covered the trip as a *Life* photographer. We had unwittingly inherited one of the best cave photographers in the country. Now the initiative was ours again—to provide the environment.

Finally the day of departure arrived, and we were off on what we hoped would be an adventure (but not too much of one).

When we arrived at the San Juan airport, we found that the car rental firm had our reservation, which they acknowledged, but they didn't have a car. This caused some scrambling, and, aided by José's knowledge of Spanish, after reaching another local car rental agency, we ended up with two cars to carry all our equipment.

Once again we had gone suddenly from hostile winter into the blinding sunlight of the tropical Puerto Rican countryside. As we drove across the causeway leaving San Juan on the military highway, we could see the modern skyline of "new San Juan" to one side, the brilliant green hills of inland Puerto Rico ahead of us, and the palm-tree-lined road luring us on. The blaring of horns and the racing of motors at intersections reminded us of home. But the pastel-colored walls of the masonry houses jarred our suburban split-level consciousness, and we were quickly brought back to Puerto Rico.

As we flashed along the gayly colored landscape, we got a hasty view of the tremendous continuing vitality and upheaval that had changed the entire culture and feeling of the island. The cars were the same—shiny American automobiles—and the gas stations, modern buildings, supermarkets, and used-car lots were direct imports from the mainland. But the advertisements heralded the marked difference. Spanish was of course used throughout the island, and the Spanish influence was seen in the architecture of the older homes—especially the iron grillwork on the fences enclosing them, and along the road in the little stores and restaurants, which displayed *chicharrones* (fried pork skins) and other foods not familiar to us.

We were traveling along the north coast highway. This main road was part of a network that completely circled the island and provided rapid surface transportation across the inland, mountainous, volcanic spine. The northern coastal plain provided a fine view of the sugarcane fields, the pineapple plantations, and the pastures dotted with fine black and white Holstein cattle. Everywhere there were people—walking, on horseback, on bicycles, or just standing at the side of the road. It was almost impossible to find a stretch of lonely road, even in areas where there may not have been a house or store visible.

A. Y. Owen, Joe Lawrence, and Jerry Frederick had not been to Puerto Rico before, and the advanced development of the island came as something of a surprise to them. Although they said nothing, I suspected they wondered how we would ever find anything not already discovered in such a densely populated

Haystack hills. *Russell Gurnee*

place. We had left the suburbs of San Juan and Bayamón behind and were in the agricultural belt, but still the land looked very civilized—not a place for exploration.

As we approached Arecibo on the north coast we were able to see the distant profile of the karst region we were to study. Scattered along both sides of the road were occasional haystacks of limestone—those curious cone-shaped hills—rising steeply out of the level, deltalike plain of the coast. These strange natural hillocks, which I had encountered on my first visit, had sheer ninety-degree walls sometimes rising one hundred feet before their sides sloped in to form their pointed tops—often two hundred feet above the plain. The sides were covered with a low, thicketlike vegetation consisting of vines, thorn bush, maguey, and, sometimes, palm trees. Occasionally the hills were pierced with cave openings—the upper part of the black openings fringed with the strange twisted stalacticites so commonly found in the entrances of tropical caves.

We stopped and photographed several of these, and it was Jerry who brought out the obvious paradox regarding the population explosion and the possibility of original exploration:

"I don't think those little caves have ever been explored." As we looked at him inquiringly, he supplied the obvious reason.

"How would you ever get up to that one over there?" he

asked as he pointed to a black opening nearly a hundred feet above us on the side of one of the ubiquitous haystacks. "It would require tension climbing, with plenty of hardware, and I don't think that that limestone is very safe for pitons." Reflecting awhile, "You might get to it from above, but how would you get to the top?"

We realized it might be possible to find a way around this hill where a rope could be dropped from the top into the cave entrance. But would anyone bother? Was it possible that here, only a few hundred feet from the main highway, we could look at the obvious entrances of caves that might be so inaccessible that they had never been entered?

As we left Arecibo we headed directly south, turning inland toward the central mountain chain. The road for the first two miles was broad and straight, climbing steadily upward toward the haystack hills. Arriving at the foot of this barrier of hills, the road began to twist and wind through the deepest part of steep valleys, circling around and around, but always climbing upward into the hills beyond. The tops of the hills were three hundred feet up; and in some of the narrow canyons followed by the road we could see the remnants of stalactites along the walls (the evidence of collapsed cave passages we discussed on our earlier visit). The area was desiccated and eroded and no longer resembled the terrain that must have existed before the caves collapsed. The road was a continuous succession of switchback turns. About eight miles in from the coast, and nine hundred feet above sea level, the land leveled off into a rolling plateau approximately three miles wide. This was deceiving as far as the underground development of the caves was concerned. One would expect that leaving the haystack hill area would signal a change of geological structure and therefore a different condition regarding the underground drainage. We were right to think so—but only in the pattern of the surface features. For this limestone was just as capable of developing caves as that farther to the north; also, this limestone was indistinguishable from that of the north.

Now the road skirted some deep ravines as we again began to rise into the uplands, increasing visibility. And although the surrounding land was relatively more level and smooth than the

Exposed cave formations in collapsed cave near Route 129. *Jeanne Gurnee*

terrain we had just left, it was by all standards of agricultural country still very rugged.

Our first stop was at the little store, or *tienda,* where we had looked down into the "bottomless" pit nearly three years before. This hole did not show on the topographic maps of the region, but it was easily located on the map by the intersection of Routes 129 and 455. We had been calling this entrance the "intersection entrance" to differentiate it from the tunnel entrance that Sixto had led us to. At José's suggestion we renamed the intersection entrance "Empalme entrance" (*empalme* means intersection in Spanish).

Nothing at the store had changed. The owner was still there, his seven children were still in Newark, and the pool table was still in use in the middle of the day. We made arrangements for some boys to help us carry our equipment into Empalme Cave the next day and drove on due south on Route 129, without the river in sight, to the "Blue Hole." This is where the

Camuy disappears underground for a mile or so upstream, or north. The hole was originally marked on a 1917 map by Bela Hubbard.

From here south the river is in view and looked about the same as on our previous trip, when we were viewing the Look-Through Cave, but it was not quite so muddy.

We had brought several pounds of fluorescein—a very powerful green dye used in the tracing of water. While A. Y. and the others went down to photograph the disappearance of the river, José and I drove farther south along the exposed route of the river to put in the dye. We wanted to determine the amount of time it would take for the fluorescein to travel a certain distance on the surface and whether it was the same river that we had seen at the bottom of the pit at Empalme. Finally, we wanted to determine how long it might take to make the traverse underground.

We drove about 1½ miles up the road, parked the car, and started walking through the sugarcane fields in the direction of the stream. We found it with no difficulty—a placid, meandering watercourse about ten feet wide. It had not rained in nearly two months, yet the water was not clear. As I poured in a one-pound bottle of dye, it took on a blood-red color from the concentrated dye and then, as the currents caught it, the stream turned a bright, fluorescent green. The water was moving more slowly than we had realized. In twenty minutes it had only proceeded about a hundred feet downstream, but by this time the whole surface was glistening green.

We strolled along, easily outwalking the flowing dye, looking for a good spot to photograph. Ahead, we could hear talking and laughter, and as we came around a sharp bend in the river we saw a dozen women standing knee deep in the stream, washing clothes on the rocks. They were startled and fell silent as we appeared. José, with a mischievous look, said to me, "We can tell them that by magic we will turn the water green in a few minutes."

The women were so stunned at seeing us, however, that he told them instead what we had done and assured them that the dye was harmless.

But we waited for nearly an hour and the color did not appear. The flow from pool to pool was so slow that the dye would take hours to reach Blue Hole. We decided to engage a small boy to notify us when the dye appeared, and we returned to the car. We drove back to meet A. Y., Al, Joe, and Jerry, who had gotten their pictures and had checked out the possibility of getting into the cave from Blue Hole.

Al assured us that access was hopeless from that direction. The entrance was one gigantic mat of logs and debris deposited by the river in flood, and the treacherous-looking mass was completely unstable—not the place to be if the river was to rise suddenly.

It was now late afternoon, and we decided that we had better make arrangements for a place to stay.

The nearest town was Lares, about ten miles inland—a beautiful place set on a high knoll. A steep road leads directly to the central plaza square where an old Catholic church overlooks the palm trees and stone benches of the park. Lares is a fine example of the colonial towns of inland Puerto Rico. Its elevation (1600 feet above sea level) gives it an invigorating climate, which accounts for the insect-free environment and chilly early mornings of winter.

We stopped to ask if there was a hotel in town, and were told there was none. José persisted, until we soon found a pension right on the square where we could get rooms. Nearby was a restaurant where we could have meals.

In a few moments the six of us had unloaded all our personal gear and were well established in the hospitality of Casa Pupilo. The mosquito-netted beds were not uncomfortable, and the cleanliness of the entire place compensated for the single shower on the back porch.

After supper we strolled around the town. The atmosphere was strange yet appealing. With the setting of the sun, the night sounds turned on full volume—the *coquí,* the familiar tree frog of the topics, the perpetual crowing of the cocks, and the blaring radios and juke boxes made it the noisiest of jungles.

We returned to the pension and during the night tried to shut out the street sounds. They never ceased.

chapter II

February 20, 1962, started out as any other sunny clear day in Lares, Puerto Rico. A lone man was sweeping the street as we went into Señor Barretta's little luncheonette. José had disappeared in the opposite direction, appearing a few moments later with a Spanish newspaper. Señor Barretta, a cheerful man, bustled about and kept busy squeezing the juice from the splendid oranges heaped up in bowls on the counter.

"John Glenn will attempt to orbit the earth today," said José as he scanned the paper.

"How would you like to be photographing that story, A. Y.?" I asked, knowing that *Life* must have a large staff covering the event.

"I wouldn't mind watching it, but from the ground," he replied. "You know, that sort of thing can get dangerous"—as if his present assignment was commonplace.

We had prepared our equipment the night before, so as

soon as we had finished breakfast we began our drive back toward the intersection of Route 129—our "bottomless" pit. We had agreed to meet our guides there and, hopefully, some boys to help us with the boats and equipment. We stopped at Blue Hole, and José went into a little house and asked about the timing of the fluorescein. The whole family came pouring out after him, each giving a separate account of how the dye had colored the whole river green. José finally broke away, gave some money to the boy who had kept the vigil, and rode on with us to the little tienda at the intersection. The owner was there, and he had rounded up half the population of the area to see us off. We got into our caving clothes and dumped all the equipment into one huge pile along the road, when José came up with the information that the river could also be seen at the bottom of another sinkhole several thousand feet south of this intersection (Empalme entrance).

The crowd was so insistent that we decided to alter our plans. It seemed worth looking into. Hopefully, it would bring us closer to our objective, an underground traverse to the Blue Hole.

We passed out all the baggage and started single file across the fields toward this new entrance. There was a definite trail, an easy hike, so we swung along with enthusiasm and interest.

Twenty minutes later we came to a fence of century plants and scrub trees on the crest of a little ridge. Several of the men took machetes and cut down the brush so that we could see beyond.

We caught our breaths as we looked into the largest sinkhole any of us had ever seen. Here, in the middle of what appeared to be rolling limestone country, was a huge, nearly circular hole more than six hundred feet across, with sheer walls extending three hundred feet below. The opposite wall was fringed with trees and vines, the white limestone exposed below and at the bottom. And, flowing across for more than five hundred feet, was the Rio Camuy.

The exit of the river was into a high, arched, black opening in the wall; its entrance into the sinkhole was obscured by feathery bamboo foliage. I lay on my stomach and looked over

the edge to a talus (scree) slope and the tops of tree ferns and green banana trees—150 feet straight down.

"How do we get down?" I asked, the same question everyone was thinking. José had already asked the men and they led us over to one side. In a few minutes the leader ducked under a single barbed-wire fence and started down a narrow two-foot-wide trail. Within twenty feet he stopped, and I saw the top of a wooden ladder as it projected above the cliff. The trail was so narrow that I motioned him to come back so that I could come down and look. When I did, I was looking at thirty feet of partially runged saplings that terminated at an impossibly narrow ledge. A few feet farther below was another ladder extending an estimated twenty feet.

"Okay, Jerry; you're the safety man on this trip," I said. "What do you think of the ladder?"

Jerry Frederick came down, took one look, and shook his head. In a few minutes he rigged one of our metal ladders alongside the sapling one. We lowered all the equipment and everyone scrambled down the ladder. We repaired the original ladder as well as we could; its rungs were made not only of saplings, but of scraps of iron and reinforcing rod—and part of a bed spring.

I was lowering some of the equipment on a rope when Joe Lawrence, who was on the metal ladder, guiding the descent, called up to me.

"Russ, those *bushes* on your right are the tops of one-hundred-foot-high trees. Be careful."

I took a book-sized slab of rock from the trail and dropped it into the "bushes." The resulting thrashing, shuddering noise made me secure myself closer to the wall as I completed lowering the equipment.

In a few minutes we were beneath a dense cover of green banana leaves. The sunlight filtering through gave an eerie jungle appearance to the entire area. The trail ahead was muddy and all the leaves and bushes were wet with condensation. This lower part of the sink was a perpetual rainforest.

<
Aerial view of Tres Pueblos sinkhole. *National Geographic Society*

Orion Knox climbing down sapling ladder into Tres Pueblos sinkhole. *Roy Davis*

The noise of the river, which had been only a whisper from the top of the ladder, was so amplified that I could not hear José—he had gone on down to the water and was shouting and waving his hands.

Although the stream was smaller than its sound had led us to believe, it was still noticeably larger than the disappearing Rio Camuy at Blue Hole upstream. When I reached José I could see it was about thirty feet wide and flowed along one wall of the sinkhole; the wall was slightly undercut by the water. Looking up—three hundred feet—we could see the overhanging trees at the edge of the sink. Only a few trees and vines clung to the chalky-white, pitted wall.

From our vantage point we could now see more clearly the outline of this enormous pit—open to the sky and pierced at the bottom by the river that flowed out from the huge arch on one side and into the smaller arch on the other.

The team assembled at the entrance of the stream, where they were climbing and transferring the equipment over the huge moss-covered breakdown, or fallen rock, to a level area. Here they could launch the boats, going against the current.

We emptied our sacks and boxes; the boys crowded around us as cable ladders, rope, life jackets, helmets, gloves, and three large yellow and blue rubber bags were spread about. Air pumps were connected, and in a few minutes the flabby rubber bags became elongated doughnut-shaped boats.

Each man, already dressed for caving, added carbide to his lamp and filled the top with water, setting the drip; as the resulting acetylene began to flow, the flames popped on.

Because this cave exploration was to be in water of unknown depth, we all put on life jackets; it is nearly impossible to swim any distance in full cave dress and heavy boots, especially in the dark.

"Who's first?" asked Al, as he threw one of the boats into the water and tied the lead rope to a rock.

"Joe and I will go first," I said. "We'd better rig up the telephone for communication on the first boat."

We were standing on a group of boulders near the water's edge, close to the natural arch of stone. Huge stalactites hung from the ceiling, curiously twisted and eroded by exposure and weathering. The sheer walls were fluted limestone, and the river flowed deep and still for at least three hundred feet to what appeared to be a bend to the right. The surface of the dark, murky stream was splattered with continuous dripping from the active formations on the ceiling.

The entrance looked so inviting and accessible that I asked José to ask the boys if any of them had ever been in the cave. One said he had swum to the far wall, "but the ceiling came down to the water—and it was too dark."

We got out our telephone equipment and Al checked the phones. Joe Lawrence stepped into the boat, kneeling and

holding it tight against the wall as I checked my lamp and stepped in.

With my full gear on, a total of 200 pounds was now centered on one foot—causing me to sink to my knee, nearly capsizing the boat. As I flopped down we drifted away from the wall. Before someone could throw down the paddles, we were swept downstream and wedged between two rocks hanging over a three-foot stretch of rapids.

<
At the bottom of Tres Pueblos sinkhole: the upstream entrance of Rio Camuy Cave. *Roy Davis*

Preparing to launch the first boat. *Roy Davis*

"You're going the wrong way, Russ," Al offered. "The cave is in the other direction."

Maintaining what dignity I could, I threw Jerry the rope at the bow of the boat and we were towed back into launching position for another start.

This time we successfully escaped the swift current near the entrance and paddled quickly upstream.

The light began to fade, and at about two hundred feet from the entrance we paused to let our eyes get adjusted to the gloom.

"There's no landing ahead," said Joe, and I realized he was talking into the phone to Al back at the entrance. I looked back and the reflection of the trees at the entrance turned the water bright green, broken only by the dripping of Joe's paddle and our sagging phone line.

We paddled on and saw that instead of a blank wall ahead, as the boy had imagined, it was a huge pile of breakdown covered with a calcite deposit, or flowstone. The ceiling rose sharply, but our lights could not penetrate the distance to estimate the height.

The river turned to the right, as we suspected, but when we began to paddle against it, the walls were closer together and the current so strong that we had to cling to the walls to pull ourselves along.

By now we were beyond the sight of light, and our earlier calm, matter-of-fact attitude began to slip away. We were no longer sophisticated, cool cavers. We were getting cave fever, and Joe's voice betrayed his excitement.

"My God, it's terrific!" I heard him say. Then, more calmly, he described to Al the width and height of the passage.

We paused and looked around the tunnel. The action of the boat caused waves, and the characteristic booming/slapping of the water trapped under overhangs and pockets in the walls was the only sound heard in the stillness.

"Ten feet wide and thirty-five feet high," Joe said, breaking the spell. And we paddled on, the route ahead, as far as we could see, smooth and open.

>

View from atop Mount Ararat as the lead boat enters Rio Camuy Cave. *Roy Davis*

A few hundred feet into the cave. *Albert Mueller*

In a few minutes we reached the end of the water passage —an oval-shaped chamber with a natural boat landing. We pulled alongside and with caution I climbed ashore and held the boat for Joe to debark.

"We're ashore and there is room for all hands," I said to Al at the other end of the phone line. "Have Jerry and A. Y. come next. We'll wait here."

"Joe," I said, "how about taking a look around—I'll wait for the next boat.

"Keep in contact," I added.

Joe checked his lamp again and started up a lead to the left.

I tied up the boat, got out my sketch pad, compass, and extra flashlight and tried to sketch what I could see—and the route we had taken. As I swung the powerful spotlight of my flash around, the room took on dimension and shape. The intriguing shadows and pockets not exposed to the dim carbide lamps were now revealed as shallow depressions or adits of the room.

I carefully estimated the ceiling height and, with great satisfaction, began my sketch map on a very small scale.

"It's going to be a big cave," I said aloud, surprising myself at the echoes I created.

The excitement of discovery and the inactivity of just sitting and waiting began to gnaw at me, so I climbed about, frequently changing my position, noting all that I could for future recollection.

At the first landing in the oval-shaped chamber. *Joseph Lawrence*

A light flooded the ceiling, and Joe popped out between two boulders almost as high. He called to me, in a voice stripped of composure.

"It goes!" he cried. Scrambling down the steep slope, he slumped down on a rock, out of breath.

"We're in the lower corner of an enormous room," Joe said, "on the side of a mountain of breakdown. The ceiling is nearly a hundred feet above us."

This from Joe, the most conservative member of the team, filled me with anticipation and impatience. As an engineer he knew dimensions and distances and as a caver he knew the curious illusions of having no scale from which to judge size.

But if Joe said it was big, it was big. I wanted to see it.

A beep from the phone interrupted us, and Al informed me that the second boat "just disappeared around the bend."

In a few seconds lights and voices came to us downstream.

A. Y. and Jerry paddled into view and came alongside the landing. We helped unload the bags and then considered our own version of a logistical problem made famous in the parlor game of missionaries and cannibals. We had two two-man boats and one one-man boat. But we had six people.

We had originally planned to leave one man at the entrance as standby, but the immensity of the cave made this unnecessary, so we could now bring everyone in.

I reported to Al on the phone: "We're sending Jerry back with the two boats. You, José, and Jerry can tow the little boat with all the equipment in it. Bring the telephone too."

A. Y. had been looking around the room while the rest of us were unloading and deciding the mechanics of transportation. I could see as I turned to talk to him that the excitement was getting to him also.

"Do you have caves like this in Oklahoma?" I asked.

"Wal," he drawled, "we got as much water—maybe not as much air."

"You haven't seen anything yet," said Joe. "You can see the entrance from up on the breakdown."

"Let's go," I said. "We'll take all A. Y.'s equipment along and get a picture of the boats coming in."

Al, José, and Jerry rejoined us and Joe and I picked up

several of the bags A. Y. pointed out. We started finding our way carefully along the route set out by Joe.

It was agreed that Jerry and José would go ahead and "bird dog" a route. Joe and I would follow, making a map, and A. Y. and Al would be last, noting the cave life, hydrology, and points of photographic interest.

José and Jerry took off, carefully toting their cumbersome rubber boat, cautious of the sharp edges of the limestone lest they tear the fabric.

I took up a station point where I could see the entrance and made a sight into the sinkhole. Then I turned around and took a sight on Joe's headlamp a hundred feet ahead in the blackness. After recording the change in compass reading on my sketch, and connecting those two points, I assumed Joe's position. He moved on and we continued the process. This crude method of surveying produces a preliminary sketch map that is invaluable as a guide, both for location and description and as a foundation on which to build the final, more accurate, report. A team of experienced cavers can survey in this manner nearly as fast as they can travel through a cave.

After three or four station points, I began to determine the shape and direction of the cave. When we emerged from the canyonlike corridors beyond the breakdown, I realized that the stream extended through a long, single corridor—one major room six hundred feet long, eighty to one hundred feet wide, and one hundred feet high. We were clambering about in a jumble at the bottom of this room, unable to see its size.

The sound of rushing water and the boom of a boat being tossed into a pool told us that José and Jerry had found the river ahead again, and after another station point we joined them at a black pool at the foot of a three-foot-high waterfall. The entire river-flow at this juncture channeled toward us through a five-foot-wide notch and spread out in a pool before disappearing off to the right in its course to the entrance to the cave.

Jerry scouted the pool to see if it was possible to portage around it, but gave up; so, while we waited, he and José paddled up to the roaring rapids.

It was impossible to ford these, so they landed on a ledge

Al Mueller climbing the obstructing waterfall in the huge room. *James Storey*

and prepared to chimney to the top of a huge boulder. Speech was impossible, but Jerry signaled from the top that it was clear ahead. We turned to go back to get our own boat when Al and A. Y. staggered up under the load of their boat, cameras, and other equipment.

We were all excited. In this enormous chamber with the roar of the river, the dripping and splashing of the water, the pristine beauty of startling white formations and blue-green rimstone pools, we were caught up in the ecstasy of original discovery.

While man's curiosity has led him to every land, under the sea, and into space, here, only a few miles from a main road in a densely populated land, we were exploring regions never before seen. As A. Y. put it, "It's strange that so much of God's beautiful work lies hidden and undiscovered."

Our zeal had gotten so great that the four of us decided to indulge ourselves. We jettisoned our camera and extraneous equipment and took only our boats, food, and safety equipment and started on foot after José and Jerry.

We caught them at the next impasse—the end of the huge room—where the river came out of what appeared to be a long tunnel and spread out around a long sand bar.

Here was a duplication of the entrance situation: a water-filled passage of unknown depth extending . . . where?

"When do we eat?" asked Al, the realist of the group, and we all realized we had had nothing to eat since seven in the morning. It was now about two thirty.

As we ate bread, cheese, and canned sausage, and drank pineapple juice, A. Y. muttered, "Why couldn't we pick out a pretty spot to eat lunch so I could take some pictures?"

"Because you haven't got your camera," I replied, and swallowed another Vienna sausage.

The inner man satisfied, we gathered on the shore, planning our next move. We decided to send both boats (we abandoned the punctured third boat) and four men ahead and have one man return from there with the boats for the other two; A. Y. and I elected to stay. Both boats cast off, paddling upstream. Left alone, A. Y. and I poked around, climbing up to look into leads and exploring around the immense room. A. Y. soon tired of this and began to choose imaginary camera angles (with an imaginary camera) while I examined the cave life in and around a dry, rimstone pool.

About half an hour later, we heard the familiar slap of paddles and soon one boat appeared, with Al in it.

"I brought back only one boat because one man can't paddle against the current up ahead," said Al. He meant that A. Y. and I in one boat could have made it, but Al, alone in the second boat, could not.

"You go ahead, Russ. I'll wait here," volunteered A. Y. Knowing that he was a seasoned spelunker, unconcerned with complete blackness around him—plus the fact that he had all the sand-

wiches—I stepped into the boat. We paddled off, leaving the sand bar and A. Y.'s light in the distance.

"What did you find?" I asked Al in the boat.

"You'll see," he said.

Oddly enough, simply not knowing what was ahead gave me the feeling of original exploration even though I knew that only a few minutes before this passage had been explored by others. Such is the simple enthusiasm of the spelunker.

As we paddled, the current against us became noticeably stronger and a breeze blew at us, suddenly increasing. My carbide light blew out, but instead of darkness, I could see a dim light ahead.

"Another entrance!" I erupted.

"It's tremendous," said Al. "Wait and see!"

We paddled faster and soon the walls and water became reflected in the dim light that now outlined the water passage. The tunnel ceiling rose to about eighty feet; ahead we could see

<
We were caught up in the magnificence of this enormous room. *James Storey*

At the first sandbar at the end of the huge room. *Albert Mueller*

the winking lights of our advance party as they climbed about in a big room ahead.

We pulled up to a sand bar and tied up alongside the other boat. The area was so light that we could clearly see the ceiling nearly a hundred and twenty-five feet above us. We climbed around a projecting rock, looked up toward the light, and saw an entrance.

The sight was breathtaking. We were at the bottom of a shaft rising at about forty-five degrees, spirally, to a fifty-foot window of blue sky and greenery. Later, measurements showed its elevation to be over three hundred feet, from water to opening. We unanimously agreed to call this the Spiral entrance (or Espiral entrance), and after a cursory exploration of the room, we returned to the boats.

The river passage extended invitingly upstream, but we decided in favor of returning to A. Y. and the main entrance. That way we could get out of the sinkhole before dark and plan our assault for tomorrow. Enroute, which was now downstream —with the current—we could have three men in a boat, which simplified travel.

We picked up A. Y. on the sand bar where we had lunched —he had lost his watch and he remarked that the wait for us seemed interminable.

We floated one boat on tether downstream, over the waterfall, to the large pool while we portaged and chimneyed along the shore. The trip back, including the ferry arrangement, worked well, and we were soon huffing and puffing up the trail out of the sinkhole just as the sun was setting.

The hotel keeper was a bit more glum than the previous day; he spotted us coming in through the side door as we tried to look casual, leaving behind a trail of muddy footprints.

Throughout the night, through supper and afterward, the exciting discoveries in the cave kept us discussing and retelling details of the trip. A sketch map from the large sinkhole to Espiral was made, and plans and a program for the next day were agreed upon.

We decided to determine the entire extent of the cave before we undertook any routine studies and observations. We were concerned that any detraction from our energy and time might cause us to miss a complete exploration. Also, we could be wasting time on places we might otherwise not consider important. Besides, here was unexplored cave, and we were there to explore it.

A team of four could most quickly and safely explore and map, we agreed, so we drew straws. A. Y. and Al became standbys.

I didn't sleep well. I reexplored the cave over and over, and a mosquito trapped inside the netting above my bed eluded me until I squashed it at about four in the morning.

By 9:00 A.M. we were again in the cave. By 11:00 A.M. we were at the foot of Espiral entrance, ready to shove off into uncharted territory.

For the third time in as many days we were looking upstream at a water-filled tunnel with no obstacles except our own limits of endurance. José and Jerry went first and Joe and I followed in the second boat.

All went well until we began to find rapids impossible to paddle against, so José, in the first boat, jumped overboard in the swiftly moving stream. In three feet of water, with a line between the boats, he waded ahead, pulling them upstream.

The rocks near the surface were now being struck by the bottom of the boats, so we all jumped over the sides and began a series of wet portages, which we alternated between short stretches of deep water.

We all were soon soaked to the neck. Periodically we emptied the boats of the gravel that poured from our boots when we crawled in and cleaned the boats with stream water. This prevented cutting their bottoms. We moved slowly in stretches of about one hundred feet so that we could map as we went. Even so, the exertions of the previous days began to tell on our strength.

The passageway continued as a narrow waterway, its walls about eighty feet straight up with no side passages, until we came to another room—identified by our reverberating shouts as a big room (which is what we named it).

We tied our boats and started up the steep flowstone and mud slope that pitched toward the river. Our flashlights were unable to pierce the interior, but when we reached our dry

Two views of Espiral entrance from below.
Roy Davis
James Storey

The Gurnees examining a curious formation in the Big Room during a later trip. *Roy Davis*

vantage point, we could see that we were in a hundred-foot-wide room at least a hundred feet high.

We climbed over the steep slope, disturbing a number of small crabs. We saw several tailless whip scorpions about ten inches in diameter. These scorpions are called *guavá* by the Puerto Ricans and are common in the caves of the island. They are reported to have a sting like a hornet, but we never heard of anyone being bitten by one.

We were now above any possible evidences of flooding, and the floor was completely unmarked by any sign that would indicate a previous entry by man. No one could possibly take this for anything but virgin cave, and we continued to be cautious, since we knew that the handholds and footholds could not have been tested or subjected to stress.

We made a sketch of the Big Room and returned to the stream, intending to follow it as far as possible. We stopped at the water's edge and refueled our carbide lamps before proceeding.

Meanwhile, Joe sat down on a large rock overlooking the river and started to empty some gravel from a boot. Suddenly there was a shout and a splash, and I saw him jump off into the river, up to his neck. I kicked one of the boats so that it swung over in front of him. He came sputtering to the surface, with a boot in his hand, grabbed the boat, and climbed ashore.

"Why did you jump in, Joe?" José asked teasingly. "It seemed to float fine." We didn't have the problem of keeping dry that we had encountered at Gage Caverns when I fell in the stream in midwinter.

Sitting around, we noticed that the eddies, pools, and waterfalls along the stream's path through the Big Room were catchalls for logs, sticks, and decayed vegetation—two miles downstream from the Blue Hole left by the risen waters of the Rio Camuy. Our interest in this trash drew a swarm of gnats (attracted by our lights) and they flew madly about, crowding one another, only to commit suicide in the flames of the carbide.

Accompanied by the odor of fried bugs, we ate a hasty meal and pushed on ahead over mountains of breakdown along the river's edge. The excitement of the day before had waned as we attempted to explore, map, and portage boats through a maze of moving-van-sized rocks. We wasted time on false leads and laborious portages until we reached open water again—and the familiar, water-filled tunnel.

But something was added. As we paddled upstream, we found a tributary coming in from a spacious side tunnel thirty feet high.

We landed on a bank and José and Jerry explored the new tunnel a little way upstream while the rest of us waited.

"It's clear and clean," José said as he returned, "and continues as far as we can see."

"It's not part of the main stream then, I guess," I said. "We'll check it out later. Let's go on ahead."

So off again—in the boats, out of the boats—until we gave up and, when the water became too deep, just draped ourselves over the sides of the boats or, when we were able to touch bottom, continued walking.

Rapids, waterfalls, sand bars, and rocks. We passed them all —until we heard the sound of a crashing waterfall louder than any we had experienced. When one is ignorant of its location and scope, the sound of thundering water in the blackness of a cave can be deceptive. The enveloping noise came from the spray of what one would expect from a giant fire hose at the side of the passage from about ten feet up and falling onto the rocks in the center of the stream. Because the falls' thin spray fanned out, it made much more noise than its volume deserved.

We were now plodding along, wading if it wasn't over waist deep, carrying the boats only if it was too difficult to push them in the water.

I took a sight ahead to where Jerry and José were now sitting in their boat. After each sight was recorded, I would blow a whistle so that they could go on. However, this time I saw them returning downstream to meet us.

"What's the matter?" I asked.

"It's a cul-de-sac," Jerry replied. "We'll have to go over or around."

We were all together now, so we concentrated our lights and began to study the area. The high, narrow tunnel was blocked by what appeared to be breakdown covered with flowstone about forty feet high. We decided to leave the boats and look for a passage over this natural but solid bridge.

In a few minutes Jerry appeared on the top of the breakdown and directed us to a route up through a crevice where we could chimney up. Soon we were all on top of this bridge forty feet above the river (and still about fifty-five feet from the ceiling).

The top of the bridge was strewn with logs and tree trunks. One trunk measured twenty feet long and ten inches in diameter, with a five-foot Y branch at one end.

"There must be plenty of big cave up ahead to permit logs like that to float through," Joe observed.

We moved along the width of the bridge, climbing over the logs and breakdown to a flowstone ledge, where we could see thirty feet below to the river. Beyond the ledge was an impassable gap. But the river was on the other side of the gap, on our level—only it was cascading into the breach, creating a noisy waterfall.

We decided to split up to find the best route for going on: Jerry and José to go back to the route we had just come from, I to the left, and Joe along the right wall.

I had not gone fifty feet when I heard that most terrifying of underground noises—a rockfall, and the thud of a boulder rolling over solid stone. The reverberation overwhelmed the roar of the river, and it was followed by a shout that cut through it all. It came from Joe's direction, partway up the right slope, but his light was hidden from me by a pile of breakdown. I called to José and Jerry as I scrambled over the rough breakdown.

My heart jumped to my throat when I saw Joe. He was standing on his head. His neck was bent at a crazy angle and his feet were straight up in the air. I ran to him and threw my arms around his legs. He groaned, "My arm."

His left arm was twisted behind him, the hand and wrist beneath an enormous boulder and he could not bend the arm to release himself from his vertical position.

Jerry arrived, saw the situation, and we braced ourselves on either side of the rock to try to lift it off Joe's wrist. We heaved together with all our strength, but nothing moved. José now arrived and the three of us tried to move the boulder. Joe gasped, so we stopped and turned our attention to him. José, a medical doctor, muttered "shock." We carefully untwisted Joe from his awkward position and placed him on his side, his arm now straight out, but with the hand and wrist still under the boulder. The rock was only four feet wide and three feet high—and of an undetermined depth. That the three of us could not move it was unnerving.

Jerry frantically began to scratch away at the dirt and rocks underneath the boulder; and we then noticed that Joe's wrist rested on a small, angular rock that sandwiched it to the big one. As Jerry removed the dirt around the small rock, it began to slip away, and José and I braced against the boulder to keep it too from sliding. Jerry carefully worked the small rock down and away, and the four of us stared in horror toward the expected injury. Slowly Joe pulled out his arm, but his hand and wrist were unharmed. Unbelievably, he wriggled his fingers. Fortunately, the small rock that had stopped the slide of the boulder had a notch in its edge the size of Joe's wrist. José examined the arm and found nothing broken.

We were badly shaken. But for an inch, Joe might have

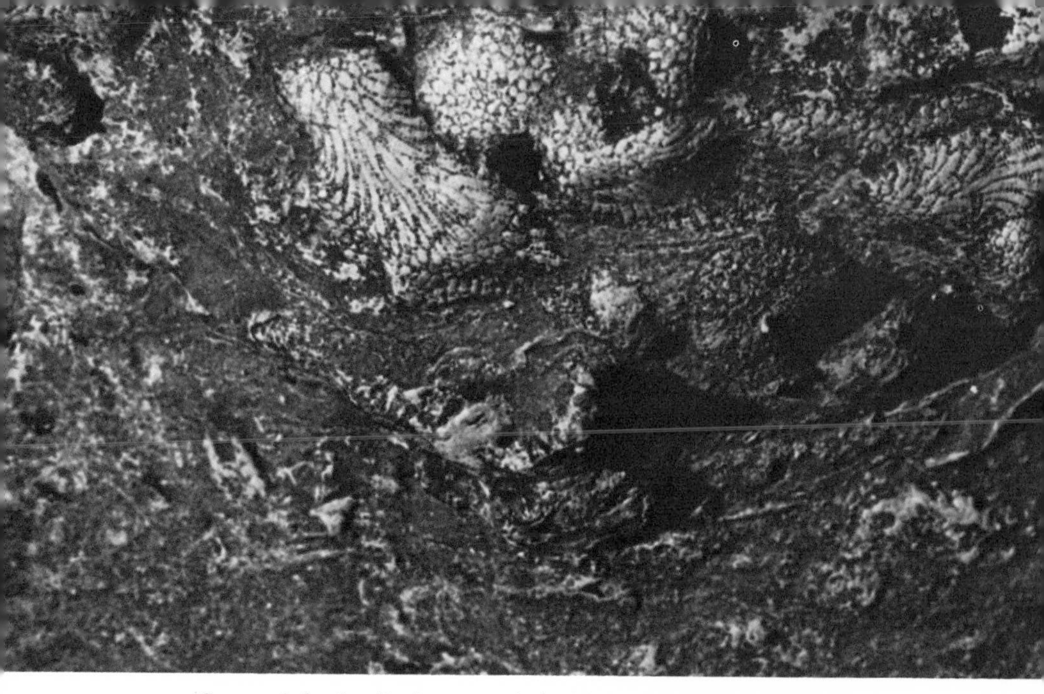

Some of the fossils that were imbedded in the walls. *José Limeres*

Left to right: Brother Nicholas, Jim Storey, and Jeff Poxon examine a rimstone pool perched atop a 35-foot-high stalagmite. *Roy Davis*

lost his hand. And considering the distance from the entrance, it might have meant his life.

We all felt we had used up our good luck for the day (perhaps the trip), and decided to quit the cave.

The next day we started out again, prepared to spend as much time as needed, wherever possible, in order to fill in the blanks on our maps.

When we reached the cave entrance, Al noted that the water had receded. The gauge we had marked on the wall the first day we arrived was about four inches above the water.

"It has gone down a little each day," said Al.

As for the flow, all our estimate could determine was that the river was still flowing at about 5,000 gallons per minute.

When we got to the oval chamber we checked the temperature, which had remained a constant 68° F. for the air and water, with a 100 percent relative humidity.

Al and A. Y., as before, had stayed behind so José took

RIO CAMUY CAVE

From Tres Pueblos Sinkhole to Natural Bridge

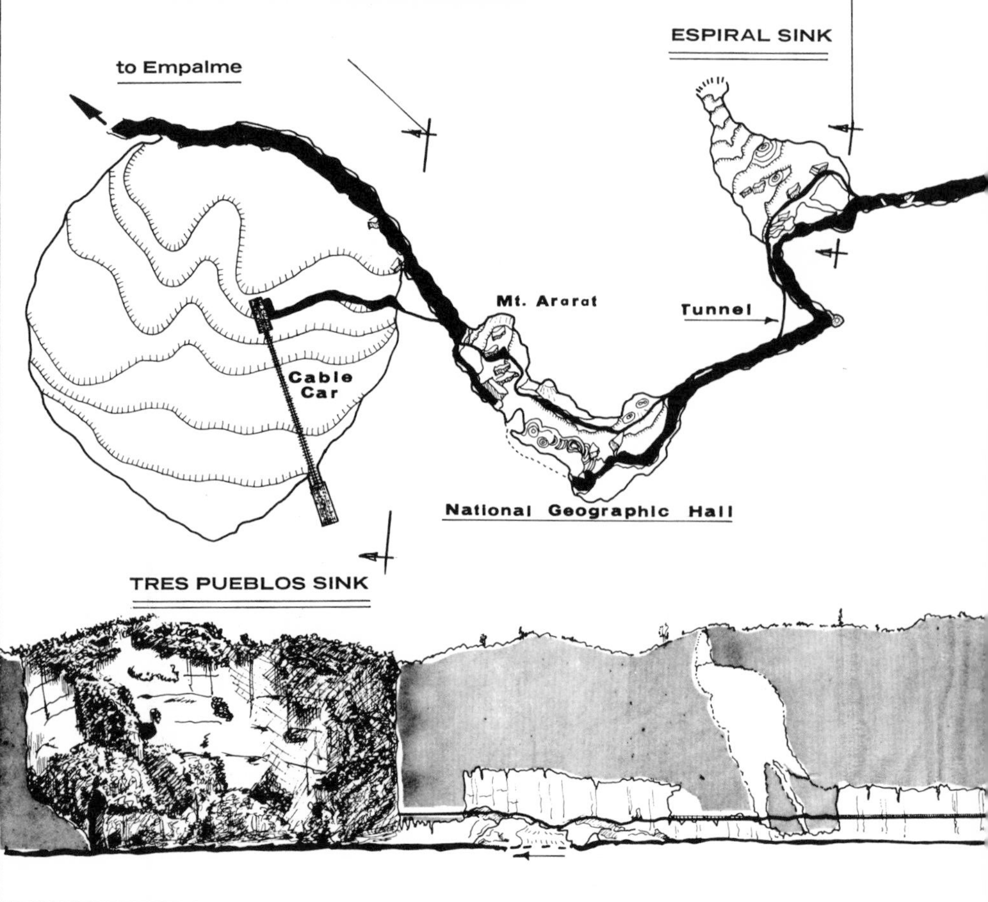

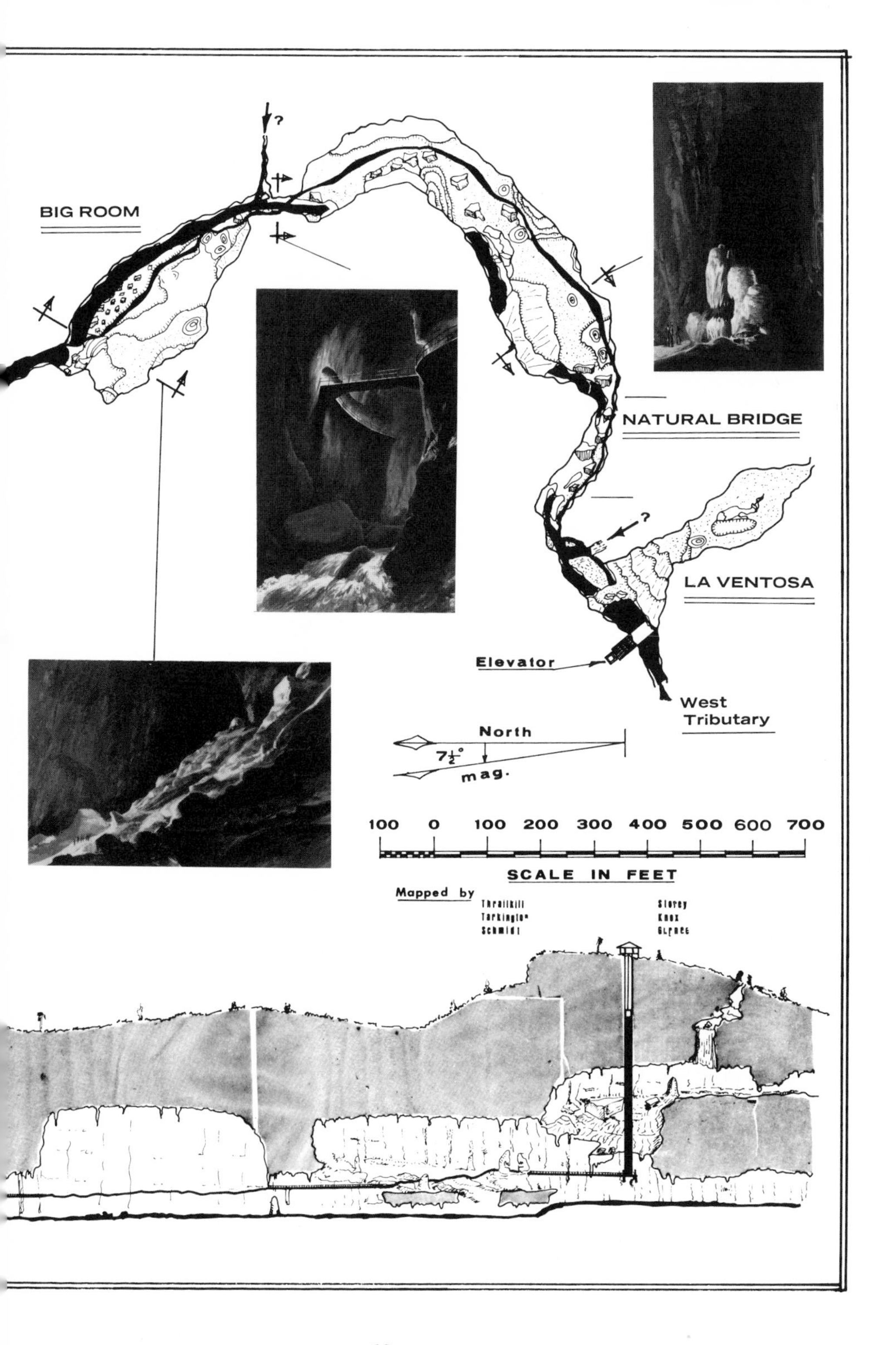

BIG ROOM
NATURAL BRIDGE
LA VENTOSA
Elevator
West Tributary
North
$7\frac{1}{2}°$
mag.
100 0 100 200 300 400 500 600 700
SCALE IN FEET
Mapped by
Thrailkill
Knox

over the photography, concentrating on fossils imbedded in the walls of the cave, while Joe, Jerry, and I explored the upper reaches of the first room to search for side passages. It was on one of these reconnaissance trips that I noticed that one of the stalagmites, rising about thirty feet from the floor, was capped with a large rimstone pool. The water was at least four feet deep —a beautiful blue-green, surrounded by a delicate lacy edge of calcite.

Two twelve-hour days were spent working our way to the Natural Bridge again. Gathering data and filling in details on the map consumed more time than we had realized. We had punctured the one-man boat, but we had become so familiar with the cave that we waded through pools rather than going to the effort of climbing in and out of the boats. The enervating environment of the cave and the daily cool "bath" began to tell on us.

Toward the end of the sixth day, I noticed that my reflexes and coordination were off; I tripped and stumbled on occasion. The rest of the team showed the same symptoms, so I decided to blow the whistle on this phase of the study.

"Tomorrow we'll check the leads on the surface around Blue Hole," I said, and there was no objection or complaint.

Our last day on the island was spent in repacking all the equipment amassed at the entrance to the cave and arranging for it to be carried back to the car. We also did some surface reconnaissance north of Empalme to look for where the river resurges and explored five little caves near the entrance to Blue Hole. All these leads proved dead, so we packed up our remaining gear and headed for San Juan and home.

To a speleologist, the results of this assault into the unknown were spectacular. We had entered, explored, and mapped virgin cave of major proportions. We had focused our attention on a single phenomenon—an underground river—and we had accomplished our mission: to provide an outstanding photographic background. A. Y. had been shooting almost continuously from the day we arrived and the complete range of activity had been covered.

chapter III

We returned to the slushy streets of New York, made our report to *Life,* and, with a bit of shock, resumed the realities of the everyday world.

The photographs were fine, the maps acceptable, and the discoveries quite unbelievable. Our report to *Life*'s Marshall Smith did not mention Joe's accident (we never related it to A. Y. Owen).

We tried to convey the size of the rooms by description, but it was not too successful. Marshall came up with a fine idea. He contracted with Mel Hunter, an excellent illustrator, to do a block diagram and a cutaway view of the cave as a two-page spread in four colors. I spent an evening with Mel; he took our maps and produced a fine bird's-eye view of the known section of the cave.

Next, the editors of *Life* felt they must have some assurance that the Rio Camuy Cave was truly unexplored (previous to our

NATIONAL SPELEOLOGICAL SOCIETY, INC.

AFFILIATED WITH THE AMERICAN ASSOCIATION FOR THE ADVANCEMENT OF SCIENCE

FROM: Russell H. Gurnee
231 Irving Avenue
Closter, New Jersey

March 13, 1962

CERTIFICATE OF VIRGINITY FOR RIO CAMUY CAVE, PUERTO RICO

Underground caverns do not require an opening to the surface in order to form. They are formed by water; and undoubtedly many thousands of caves exist that have no surface entrances. Most speleologists state as a requirement of definition that a cave be large enough to provide access of a person. It should also be formed by natural processes and be deep enough to exclude all external light.

A cave never visited or explored by humans is considered a virgin cave, even though it may contain surface debris brought in by water or gravity from the outside. Determination of previous exploration can usually be clearly shown by footprints or marks unnatural to a cave. In certain caves in France such fragile evidence as the bare footprint of prehistoric man has been perfectly preserved in the plastic mud floor for nearly 20,000 years. Equally remarkable claw marks and hair from the extinct cave bear are also found in these same caves.

The Rio Camuy Cave in Puerto Rico, explored south from the Tres Pueblos entrance was at the time of the N.S.S. Field Trip of February 16, 1962, a virgin cave. This information was obtained from geologic reports, observation and personal correspondence.

Local inquiries strengthened the reports that no one had ever explored the underground course of the Rio Camuy. Personal talks with town officials, local geologists and property owners all assured us that no one had ever entered beyond daylight in the upstream section of the cave.

The Rio Camuy Cave has been very kind to the members of the National Speleological Society, and it would be ungentlemanly of us to question her virginity. It is therefore declared that to the best of our knowledge, the report of the N.S.S. Field Trip dated February 16-24, 1962, is the first visit and exploration ever made by man. The sketch map prepared is the only record published of this specific portion of the subterranean Rio Camuy.

Russell H. Gurnee

Russell H. Gurnee

President

DEDICATED TO THE EXPLORATION, STUDY AND CONSERVATION OF CAVES trip) and that we were, without a doubt, the first to enter this major cave system. I prepared an affidavit—probably the first Certificate of Virginity for a cave ever issued. It seemed to satisfy the editors, and soon the page proofs were ready and we were looking forward to a publication date.

The article was not to be published, however. It was preempted by a story submitted at the same time by Erle Stanley Gardner (of Perry Mason fame) about a cave in Baja California which he discovered by helicopter. Its unusual feature was a series of Indian pictographs that covered the walls. His story was accepted and, since it was too soon to run another cave story, our efforts never reached print. There was an interesting footnote. The week following the publication of Gardner's cave story, there was a letter to the editor from an archaeologist who stated that the Indian paintings had been known for years—that they were discovered by Spanish explorers in the seventeenth century!

So we were adrift again with our Puerto Rican cave; and strangely enough, I began to doubt its gigantic size. Perhaps it was not the major discovery I had thought. My wife, Jeannie, and I had been caving for about twelve years, and even though we had visited over a thousand caves, was it possible I had overestimated the scale of the Rio Camuy in comparison with the others?

We had visited most of the largest tourist caves in the United States, including Carlsbad, Mammoth, Luray, Cumberland, and Marvel, but not one was like the Rio Camuy. The river added that exciting dimension.

We had been in caves in tropical areas—Venezuela, Mexico, Guatemala, El Salvador, and on the Caribbean Islands, but these also did not measure up to the Camuy.

We had seen Padirac in France, which is somewhat reminiscent of the Rio Camuy in that it has an active river and fine large rooms. As a show cave, Padirac is entered by elevator, is traversed by boat, and ends in a huge, domed room. It was discovered and explored by the great French speleologist Edouard-Alfred Martel in 1895 and has attracted millions of visitors in the years since.

Travels to Spain, England, Wales, Austria, Switzerland, and Germany did not reveal caves similar to the Camuy.

In Yugoslavia we had seen some of the finest caves in the world. Postojna and Skocjanske Jame were particularly outstanding. The latter swallowed up an entire river, which flowed beneath limestone and reappeared in the water supply of the city of Trieste, many miles away. We had visited the cave three days after it had flooded. The water level was then normal and the water was flowing quietly at the bottom of a huge room one hundred feet wide and nearly three hundred feet high. A narrow iron suspension bridge two hundred feet above the water spanned the gap between the walls. The guide showed us the water line at the height of the flood—twenty feet over the bridge! There may be larger underground rivers yet to be discovered, but for sheer dramatic impact, Skocjanske Jame had all the ingredients to make it one of the world's most exciting caves, and perhaps the only rival for the Rio Camuy.

But while I was seeking reassurance of my impression of the Camuy's size, Jeannie, who had heard me talk so much about it, had never seen it. We decided to make a survey trip with our friends John Spence, Al Mueller, and José Limeres.

In the meantime, my report of the *Life* trip had been published in the National Speleological Society's monthly publication. We sent copies to the Puerto Rican authorities who might be interested in our discovery.

One of the most enthusiastic men who corresponded with me at that time was Dr. Rafael Picó, then president of the Banco Gubernamental de Fomento. He was a geographer by training and sent me publications of his work on the island. I wrote to him that the Rio Camuy should be set aside as a park and preserve to avoid its becoming vandalized and possibly contaminated. My suggestion received enthusiastic response—courteous letters—but no concrete action. It appeared up to us to create a definite plan showing how the cave could be developed (so that a portion of it could be shown to visitors)—the major part left for future generations to study and explore.

I was a little frustrated and anxious that the area be protected. I wrote to Rafael Limeres (José's father), in San Germán, asking him if he could locate the owner of the land that encompassed the Empalme entrance.

I began to think of the people who lived on the land above the cave and realized that I did not know much about them. We had always traveled in a group, and José usually did all or most of the talking. Only he got to know the men who accompanied us cutting trails through the undergrowth, around the cave entrances, and who sometimes followed us inside with torches or flashlights.

When Señor Limeres wrote to me that he had gone to the cave on September 1, 1962, and had talked to the owners of the cave property, I suddenly got a different viewpoint of the life that went on only a few hundred feet above the cave system we had discovered.

Señor Limeres took immediate and enthusiastic interest in the caves of the Camuy. He was fiercely proud of his island and excited about the possibility that the Rio Camuy would some day be an outstanding attraction. He was born in San Germán, educated in the local schools, and, upon graduation from high school, won a scholarship to Park College in Missouri. When he graduated, he returned to Puerto Rico and became a high school teacher. His forty years with the local school system had made him well known, respected, and popular with generations of young people. A short, stocky, energetic man in his early sixties, he had a vital interest in all about him.

Later he arranged for a real estate agent to go with him to the caves and wrote me of his findings:

"According to Mr. Longoría, the local broker, all these lands are very poor, with little good soil and plenty of rock formations, no good for agriculture or grazing, but the climate is very convenient for old and retiring peoples. He estimated that the price of these lands should be between $100 and $200 per acre (no more); but since these farms are located or border on a paved road like Road No. 129, the price may be a little higher."

He met and spoke with the owners of the farms that provided access to the cave entrances and asked them if they would sell their lands. This met with varying responses. "Not for any amount of money. I have lived here for a good number of years; I like the place and I intend to remain here," said Francisco Roman Vera, owner of seventeen *cuerdas* (a *cuerda* is a little smaller than an acre) that included the entire Empalme entrance. Lalo Vasquez, who owned the Espiral entrance, said he would not sell his farm, but that he would part with a narrow strip of land on the side of the ravine as an access. About the price, he would want to know how much land was wanted. Both these men were actively farming the land. At least they were cultivating what small portion of it they could to produce squash, coffee, oranges, and other products. Livestock consisted of several cows and some pigs.

The most interested owner was Confesor Rodriguez (popularly known as Sonny Rodriguez), a farmer and merchant. He owned twenty-two cuerdas and the ravine that led down to the Empalme entrance. He was willing to sell if the price was agreeable.

All the above information, combined with sketch maps that Señor Limeres had carefully colored to distinguish the farms, gave me some idea of the relationship of the surface ownership to the cave below. It also put some "flesh" on an area I had considered merely rocky, tropical terrain. I was fascinated that these farmers, who had spent most of their lives in the area, had never been in the caves. I began to wonder. Had their curiosity never been aroused? Might some of them have gone into the Rio Camuy? Señor Limeres asked the local people on each of his return trips, but no one knew of any exploration.

The development of the entire area had lagged behind other, more metropolitan parts of the island. Before the Lares-Arecibo roadway was completed in 1920, all the produce of the farms was brought to market on mules or horses. And though the completion of the road opened up access to the rock-bound land, installation of a city water supply was not completed for inhabitants near the Rio Camuy Cave in 1962, the year of our visit. Water had been carried from little nearby springs, or one walked about 2½ miles down the road to the nearest roadside spigot.

I was convinced that the opening of the cave to the public would be a boon to the economy of the region. But I was concerned about the possibility of the pollution a large, transient population would create—and also the inevitable commercial satellite enterprises that always surround such a successful venture. I might in the long view be causing the destruction of the very thing we had set about to preserve—the beautiful environment of the Camuy.

The only solution was to visit the cave again, this time with Jeannie and our friends, to survey and photograph the surface and find a way to retain the natural beauty of the area.

In November 1962, we were again at the Casa Pupilo in Lares listening to the Puerto Rican night noises and looking down from the hotel balcony at the town square. The young girls and boys were promenading in the early evening and the older people sat on stone benches talking.

Early the next morning, while the mist was still rising off the cliffs, Señor Limeres called on us at the hotel, and we were soon driving along Route 129 under the long branches of flamboyant trees.

The markings on the rural roads were invaluable for locating the trails and landmarks in our quest for the caves. Kilometer posts (a kilometer equals 0.6 of a mile), incised with the kilometer reading, are placed every 100 meters (a meter equals slightly more than a yard) along the roads. The numbers start from one town and end at another. The Arecibo-Lares road begins at 0 kilometers in the town square at Arecibo and ends at 33.9 kilometers in the plaza at Lares. This provides an excellent rural address system, accurate to within one hundred meters.

We watched the descending kilometers along the familiar Route 129: K24 (the little house where we had changed clothes to see La Cueva del Humo, K23.6 (Look-Through Cave), K23.2 (Blue Hole), K21.2 (Sonny Rodriguez's store). We looked for a place to park the car but the shoulders were too narrow. At K21 we found a space large enough.

We spread out a topographic map of the area on the hood of the car and located our position. The houses showed as black squares, while dotted lines branched off the main road, representing foot trails to other houses farther off the road.

Señor Limeres obtained directions to the house of Juan Velez, one of the landowners, and we all started off down the road to a trail we were to take. Al and John were taking pictures of the panorama, and Jeannie was admiring the unfamiliar flowering trees and the bushes and plants along the trail. We went over a ridge and past a small pigpen, following the contours of the slope toward the area of the underground Rio Camuy. Señor Limeres was delighted with Jeannie's interest in the native plants and proceeded to give her a running commentary of the many varieties. He would pick a leaf here, caution about the spines of another, or strip a twig off one for her to taste. I glanced back at the trail and found that we had acquired a gaggle of small children.

Juan Velez's house was like many in the area—of wood construction with a pitched corrugated iron roof. It was partly hidden behind a huge breadfruit tree that grew alongside it, and a planting of maguey completely encircled the house, serving as an effective fence to keep livestock in or out. Just inside a gate was a curious low A-shaped corrugated roof that seemed to be lying directly on the ground. I asked Señor Limeres about this structure and he said it was a hurricane shelter. I glanced at the clear blue sky (only a few puffy white clouds were off on the horizon) and realized there was more to this idyllic climate than met the tourist's eye. It could be a hard life wrenching a living from this rocky, thin soil, nearly impossible to plow. Machinery was useless—there was not enough level land, and the crops we could see were those raised only for their own consumption. Squash, beans, corn, melons, and peppers were growing in a little garden next to the house. We had seen some of the neighbors' crops—breadfruit, oranges, grapefruit, coffee, sugarcane, and tobacco—but these were grown in small quantities in the pockets of suitable soil, remote from one another and difficult to transport.

Señor Velez was at home and came out to meet us. He was a small man, slender and deeply tanned. Although his face was lined, and hair quite gray, he appeared to be in his thirties. He carried a machete, which is customary in rural Puerto Rico.

He greeted Señor Limeres cordially, and when introduced to each of us he shook hands with that characteristic lifeless grasp I always seem to experience with farmers everywhere. Señor Limeres talked with him in Spanish (Velez spoke no English), asking him about his property. Velez waved the machete in the general direction of the trail we had come from and then swept it around in a half circle, indicating the boundaries of his land.

We learned that Velez owned about three cuerdas along the ridge we crossed to get to his property and that he farmed all the tillable soil of the big sinkhole we had explored for *Life*. That he farmed it was something of a surprise, but this is where he grew bananas and plantains.

A section of the topographic map had been enlarged to scale so that the houses and trails could be easily identified. We spread the map on the ground and, with the help of Velez, located the property of his immediate neighbors. Velez's sinkhole was clearly shown on the enlarged map but it appeared at the intersection of three towns: the municipio de Camuy to the north, the municipio de Hatillo to the east, and the municipio de Lares to the west. Our first reaction to this was that the sinkhole (which had no local name) should be called the Triboro Sink. However, this did not seem fitting for the area, so José suggested the Spanish equivalent—Tres Pueblos Sink.

Velez explained that the sink was a separate farm and that he had a deed for it. It consisted of six and one half cuerdas. Jeannie, who had not visited these parts before, was eager to see everything at first hand, so we folded the map and asked Velez if he would take us to the rim of the sink so that we could look for the town intersection markers.

We started off on one of the numerous trails leading through the high shrubs that extended beyond the maguey. It was more like a procession now, for all the neighborhood children had gathered as we single-filed toward the Tres Pueblos Sink.

We had not approached the sink from this direction before and were surprised to have it appear suddenly in front of us. Jeannie gasped; I had the enjoyment of pointing out to her the river below and the little trail that permitted access to it. Velez was busy slashing at the underbrush near the rim of the sink—so that we might get a better view, I thought. But when he called I knew he had been looking for something. It was a cement monument marking the intersection of the three towns. We spread our maps again and with a compass were able to position ourselves with no difficulty.

I had not realized the complex system of property lines that had been developed over the years. The description of the Tres Pueblos Sink property stated that it was owned by Juan Velez, bounded on the east by the property of Confesor Rodriguez, on the north by Francisco Roman, on the west by José Raices, and on the south by Millan Fazques. This would seem to leave the exact boundaries up to the individuals named—probably satisfactory for agricultural use of the land. But we could imagine the complications that might arise with the consideration of subterranean rights. Add to this that lawfully all the rivers of the island are public domain and under the control of the Commonwealth, and the possible problems become still greater.

Now that we had examined both the surface and underground areas, we could see the benefits in opening up the Rio Camuy Cave. We had found a resource for this undeveloped part of the island that, properly protected and developed, would change the economic and social conditions of the entire region. I recalled an account I once read of a visit to the valley of the Yellowstone in the last century by a group of businessmen from Montana, who made the first survey of that remarkable area. They recognized the great importance of that scenic beauty spot and decided to work for its establishment as a park. Today Yellowstone National Park is larger than the island of Puerto Rico.

In Puerto Rico, the spot we had found was small in comparison, but the circumstances were the same. The Rio Camuy environment was unique and deserving of protection. Our party agreed that we would try to encourage the government to recognize the uniqueness of the cave so that the Camuy might have perpetual protection.

We returned with Velez to his house and were invited in for coffee. His wife had anticipated our coming, and the living room was set up for guests. A bright-colored cloth covered the square table, and wooden chairs and a bench were set for us.

Jeannie particularly appreciated the fare, for as we sat and talked she noticed that the refreshments were all products of the little farm we were visiting. The coffee, black and steaming, came from the berries grown in the shady grove behind the house; the sugar, from the few stalks of cane we had seen near the fence; the milk, from one of Velez's several meandering cows; and the fruits, which we found exotic, probably from the sinkhole.

After our repast, as we prepared to take our leave, I took out my pipe. But Velez was ever the constant host. He anticipated my move, suggested some of his homegrown tobacco, placed a piece outside on a block of wood, and, with his machete, chopped it up for my pipe. We left savoring his hospitality and cordiality.

In the several days remaining of this trip, Al Mueller and I did a rough survey of a possible roadbed from Route 129 into the area of the cave; John Spence took photographs, and Jeannie chatted in Spanish with the children and ladies. Our notes and pictures resulted in a proposal to the Puerto Rican government on December 11, 1962. We called it *Proyecto Rio Camuy: A Development Plan for Rio Camuy Cave—Proposed Park and Recreation Area,* and directed it to Rafael Picó, Robert Bouret, the director of tourism, and other interested government officials. It read in part:

"This proposal is made to provide an outline for suggested development of the cave and surrounding surface area as a park, recreation area, and tourist attraction for the people of Puerto Rico and visitors to the island."

Receipt of the proposals was acknowledged, and now we waited. I was not too optimistic. I felt there was interest but perhaps not enough for anything to be done about the protection of the area.

My pessimism must have been sensed by Señor Limeres. He wrote to me:

"I took a little time in answering your kindly letter, always hoping to send you good news about the caves. I think you should not give up the idea of furthering the project no matter how many difficulties you find in your way to success. DON'T GIVE UP is a phrase heard and followed by many of the big successful men of this age.

"In my personal opinion I dare to suggest that buying the 20-acres [sic] farm from Don Confesor Rodriguez will give you a control of almost the whole project without danger of future interference by any person or group of persons interested in promoting the project. The price is $4000, I think, which is not too high for land in Puerto Rico."

I could see why Señor Limeres had been a successful teacher, and I could imagine the number of students who were inspired by his enthusiasm. But my proposal had been made to the government, and so, on January 11, 1963, I answered his letter as follows:

"There is at this time no particular advantage for me to purchase Sr. Rodriguez's property. I do not believe there is much speculative value to it and control of it would not serve any particular purpose—unless I were wealthy enough to purchase it and donate it to the Government."

However, Señor Limeres was right. After considerable correspondence, he knew that my protests and attempts at patience were primarily bravado. When nothing was heard by May, I permitted Señor Limeres to pursue an agreement with Sonny Rodriguez to purchase his farm—the land that controlled access to all three cave entrances.

This decision included the intention of another exploration, in February of 1964, this time with a larger team which might push on beyond where Joe Lawrence had his accident. I felt happy that something was happening. Planning for the trip buoyed my interest as I concentrated on the preparations for a major expedition.

All this pleased Señor Limeres, and he quickly obtained an option to buy the land. He wrote:

"On Sunday, May 26, my brother, two witnesses and myself went to see Don Confesor Rodriguez. We did not find him at his home but finally located him at a place called Angeles, near the town of Utuado. I took a typewriter with me so as to be ready for action. For about half an hour we tried to convince him for selling for $3500.00 but he was not willing to. Finally he was willing to sell both farms (the 20 acres and the 2½ acres) for a price of $4000."

With this agreement in the very capable hands of Señor Limeres and his brother, Luis Angel Limeres, I felt that all would proceed. I prepared a proposal to The Explorers Club in New York and the National Geographic Society in Washington, applying for financial aid for an expedition. The trip would also be an official expedition of the National Speleological Society.

On September 17, Señor Limeres, with a power of attorney, purchased the property from Sonny Rodriguez. Now, for better or worse, I was committed to a financial as well as a personal interest in the Rio Camuy caves.

I began to think of the personnel for the coming trip. We already had a nucleus of experienced men who knew the area: Al Mueller, Joe Lawrence, Jerry Frederick, and José Limeres. All of them were able and qualified to be leaders of teams into the cave. But we did not have enough specialists to provide the type of coverage I felt would make the study of significant value.

A solution was to provide open applications for these posts to everyone in the National Speleological Society. An announcement in the national newsletter brought more than fifty applications for the unfilled positions on the team. This included the fields of geology, biology, surveying, photography, and so on. I did not have the temerity to select the team myself, so a committee of four made the final choice.

The bulk of the initial preparations fell to Jeannie: the voluminous correspondence with the Puerto Rican government and possible sponsors, applications, and progress and equipment reports to the team. It was absolutely necessary that each detail be exactly right—sleeping accommodations, food, a central point for group meetings, and so on—in order to ensure that team morale would be kept high during the time of the explorations. Failure in any of these could reflect in the amount and quality of work we would be able to accomplish. Twenty-two acres of hills, sinks, and thick undergrowth would have to be modified to accept and serve this invasion of cavers. There were no adequate accommodations that we knew of, so Jeannie and I decided on a reconnaissance trip to set up a headquarters.

Thanksgiving week, 1963, found us back at "K20" on the Lares road. Previously, Sonny Rodriguez had mentioned a little house on the property, but we had never seen it. Now we were to make a tour. The trail to the house, about a thousand feet from the road, was overgrown, and Sonny went ahead swinging his machete to clear away the undergrowth. We crossed several fences and then came to a small green rural house (a *casita*) that belonged to Sonny's mother but which was now unoccupied. It was shining-clean, no cobwebs, and light and airy—in arrangement very much like others in the area, with one room in front

Our headquarters house. *Russell Gurnee*

and three in back (one of these would become our kitchen). Since the whole building was not more than 14 feet by 25 feet, it would not be too roomy inside, but certainly ample for our purposes.

I turned to Sonny and, through Señor Limeres, who had met us there, asked how much he would like for the house.

"Make an offer," he replied.

"Two hundred dollars," I said.

Sonny nodded and we shook hands, while Jeannie was already examining the little dwelling with the eye of an interior decorator.

There was much to be done to make it ready for the expedition. Sonny agreed to provide a barrel, which would serve as a cistern for wash water; and we would install the gutters. And although the outside power lines had been disconnected, the house had been wired for electricity. I made a careful survey and decided that we had a good bargain.

Sonny then took us for a tour of part of our property. We saw a sinkhole near the house almost a hundred and fifty feet deep. Jeannie and I tossed in rocks and counted the seconds till they crashed at the bottom. Another mystery hole to be explored.

At the edge of a ravine was a cattle trough supplied by drainage from the roof of the cow shed. A little farther on we came to several orange trees laden with ripe fruit. Sonny shook a tree, selected two oranges, and, with his two-foot machete, prepared them for us in perfect spiral pealings.

After that, and for the entire week, instead of lounging on the beaches like any reasonable visitors to Puerto Rico, we spent our time with hammers, nails, saws, paint, and hardware.

With the help of Sixto Irrazi, our guide on previous expeditions, who now joined us as painter, the roof became a fine red, the outside walls gray (heretical in Puerto Rico), and the trim white. New glass was installed in the windows, and the floor no longer sagged. And we had a galvanized sink, which was connected to the rain barrel (which had no water yet). We were about as civilized as we could hope to be after only a week's work.

Jeannie and I returned home to learn that The Explorers Club had approved our grant application. This was followed in a few days by the acceptance of our proposal to the National Geographic Society. We were elated.

Now the expedition lacked for only one thing: We would need a cook. The solution came through a Cave Capers outing in Indiana that I had attended a few months earlier. I had seen a young man dressed in a white apron who was working behind a charcoal grill in the campground parking lot. He was cooking chicken, and the pungent aroma caused me to pause and watch him. He misinterpreted my actions and speared a chicken leg with his fork and offered it; he had no way of knowing that I abhor chicken. I couldn't refuse—and found it delicious. His name was Jeff Poxon, a high school student whose hobby was cooking. But he was also an amateur wrestler and a caver. At seventeen, he certainly had a variety of interests (and I was intrigued with his expertise with the chicken). And while I watched him the next morning making popovers in a field oven, we talked again and he showed me his box of condiments and collection of knives and chef's kit.

Now I offered the job to him and his acceptance completed our roster for the expedition.

chapter IV

The team had been selected, plans were completed, plane tickets were mailed, and equipment was shipped. There were sixteen of us:

David S. Boyer, photographer (National Geographic Society)
Roy A. Davis, explorer
Jeanne Gurnee, logistics and, later, editor of publications
Russell Gurnee, leader of expedition
Joseph Lawrence, leader of Team II
José Limeres, doctor and explorer
Albert C. Mueller, communications and explorer
Brother Nicholas Sullivan, biologist
Jeffrey Poxon, cook
Victor A. Schmidt, surveyor and explorer
John Spence, supply
James Storey, rope work and explorer
Terry Tarkington, surveyor and explorer
John Thrailkill, geologist
Leovigildo Vásguez, consulting geologist in San Juan
Arlan Wiker, photographer (National Geographic Society)

On February 8, 1964, we all assembled at the headquarters house. Hundreds and hundreds of pounds of equipment were scattered about in mounds in the front yard. In the middle of it all was John Spence, sitting in an inflated yellow and blue rubber boat and carefully swabbing the sides with a shaving brush full of soap.

"I think I've found another leak," he said. "We'll have to check all the old boats carefully before we can use them."

These were the boats that had been used on the first expedition. John and I had come to the island a few days early in order to complete the odds and ends necessary before the arrival of the main team. With everyone assembled, the house suddenly looked too small for the group, but the addition of several tents which we set up under breadfruit trees nearby eased the congestion.

This arrangement left us with a house that would sleep half the team and accommodate a rather claustrophobic kitchen, laboratory, study, and dining hall for all.

Over a fine supper by the light of gasoline lanterns, we had our first relaxed moment for team members to become acquainted. Even though I was the leader, I knew some of the members only through correspondence. It was my first meeting with Terry Tarkington, an engineer from Alabama and a fine cartographer, and Jim Storey, a civil engineer from Georgia, who would be in charge of rope work and rigging. All of us were meeting for the first time Dave Boyer and Rick Wiker, the photographers from the National Geographic Society.

An important ingredient for success on a trip such as this is the rapport that must exist among individual members. This would be keenly felt as we shared the rigors and discomforts of exploration and camping—which included hauling almost all our water from an outdoor town spigot four miles away and carrying food and supplies on foot over the trail to the house.

Dave Boyer asked me how the team had been chosen, and I explained that we had requested applications from the membership of the National Speleological Society, regardless of geographical location, in order to assemble the best team possible.

"A committee finally made the selection from fifty applicants," I said.

And Joe Lawrence added, "And we were the ones who lost."

That evening our overall plan was made. We divided the starting group into two teams of four, while geologist John Thrailkill and the biologist, Brother Nicholas, would be free agents about the area. The primary purpose was to explore and map as much of the underground route of the river as possible. Brother Nicholas would be on call to examine any new species that might be discovered; John Thrailkill would study the geology to help reconstruct the topography of the area and the manner in which the cave was formed.

Joe Lawrence and I would lead our teams separately at first and then jointly in the areas we might discover.

Team I consisted of José Limeres, doctor; Vic Schmidt, surveyor; Roy Davis, group photographer; and myself. We were going to go into the Tres Pueblos entrance and push on to the Natural Bridge.

Joe Lawrence, Al Mueller, Terry Tarkington, and Jim Storey as Team II had several jobs. They would leave at the same time as I and were to rig the Espiral Sink, as ladders and ropes at this entrance would permit us a shorter trip to the river. They were also to try out two-way radio contact from the cave to headquarters. When they returned to the house, they would explore the pit near it as well as any other leads on the surface.

Early the next morning I left with Team I for the Tres Pueblos entrance. While they had studied the maps and reports, this would be Vic and Roy's first sight of it. Vic wrote in the trip log that night:

> What impressed me most as we came over the lip of the enormous Tres Pueblos sink was not the size of the depression, which is certainly gigantic, but the sight of a small banana plantation 250 feet down. I kept thinking of the Puerto Rican farmer who would have to carry the fruit up the steep path and makeshift ladder. But then I saw the entrances and the swift stream coming from one black hole into the sunlight, only to vanish again into another.

<
Mealtime in the casita. *Roy Davis*

Roy Davis was also impressed with the sight. In addition to being the group photographer, he is also one of the most experienced and agile cavers in the country. We carried the equipment down the steep trail to the river bank, then upstream over the slippery rocks toward the entrance, where Roy had problems. This is what he wrote in his report:

> Tragedy befell me as we approached the upstream entrance with the first boat. My ankle caught between a couple of rocks; and as my weight was placed on the left foot, it slipped, banging the little toe (inside the shoe) against a projection. Woe of woes, the darned toe bent backwards and popped. That ended my caving for the day—and several days thereafter.

José confirmed that Roy had broken his toe. We hadn't even gotten into the cave and we had a casualty! Roy was chagrined, but he gave his spot to John Thrailkill, the expedition geologist, and limped off back to camp.

After this unfortunate beginning, we turned our attention to the cave ahead and prepared to launch. José and Vic went first, and John and I prepared to follow. Vic described his first experience:

> We shoved off paddling against the stiff current. We were immediately working fairly hard, but I did have a chance to glance back at the sight of the brilliantly lit entrance, crowned with massive stalactites and draped with moss and vines.

John, who was not scheduled to go into the cave, luckily had his hard hat and carbide lamp with him. We borrowed Roy's life jacket and I adjusted the webbed straps to fit John. No one liked wearing these gray, horse-collar, navy-issue jackets because they are uncomfortable for doing any strenuous work. But I insisted that we take this precaution while in the boats and river.

John and I are both about six feet five, so it was with some difficulty that we collapsed our frames into the boat and pushed off after José and Vic.

When we arrived at Espiral entrance, we could see Joe, heading Team II, descending the last few feet of a steep flowstone bank. They had successfully rigged that entrance, and he was now trying out the two-way radio with Al Mueller at the surface. The reception, though, only seemed to be good in direct line of sight; subsequently we did not use this mode of communication.

We arranged with Joe to leave Espiral entrance rigged with a stainless steel ladder so that we would not have to go back out the Tres Pueblos entrance when we returned. I told Joe my team was going to go as far as possible beyond the Natural Bridge and that we might be gone all night, and that no one need be concerned about us until the next morning. If we didn't return by that time he was to send a second team after us. Joe agreed and started back up the steep climb at Espiral, toward headquarters.

The trip upstream to the Big Room was as we remembered it. The water flowed so swiftly between the sheer eighty-foot walls that we could not paddle against it. Often we were out of the boats, wading and splashing ahead until the water got too deep, when we would flop back in again. In some places we would pull ourselves along the fluting of the walls.

We took the lower, most direct route through the Big Room, portaging our inflated boats up and over the huge breakdown slabs that slowed our movements. José noted in the log:

> The Big Room appears to have gained in size and has plenty of gnats, or some such annoying insects. They enter your nose, mouth, ears and occasionally burn in your carbide flame with a peculiar burnt-flesh odor. A small bodied, long legged little spider climbed on me on the way out of the Big Room.

While José obviously had been troubled by the Big Room, apparently Vic and John at the time were so busy with the mechanics of getting over and around the breakdown that they did not mention the room in the log at all.

We soon stopped to eat a late lunch and then looked about the section on top of the Bridge, musing over the rock that had so nearly trapped Joe. The waterfall was just as noisy and looked just as impossible to climb. Again we looked for an alternate route ahead.

The solution was so simple that we could hardly imagine we could have missed it the first time. The left wall flanking the Natural Bridge led directly to a pool above the waterfall. Within seconds we were beyond the earlier explored portion—and in virgin cave. The pool water flowed off to one side and thundered over to create the waterfall, and the main passage ahead once again stretched into the blackness.

We launched our boats into the still, deep water of the passageway, now some fifty feet above the previous water level, fifteen to twenty feet wide. The ceiling height exceeded one hundred feet, its dripping water splattering us, and occasionally we were treated to a shower-bath spray from the overhanging formations.

As a geologist, John was intrigued with and sketched and took measurements of a large stalagmite that nearly blocked the passage. At one point it dammed up the river so that a small waterfall flowed around one side. The possibility of a huge ten-foot stalagmite mound forming while water coursed around it seemed impossible, since stalagmites must form in the air with dripping water.

Our appetites even for this most remarkable underground passage began to wane when our legs began to cramp from kneeling in the boats. And we wondered if we were going to be able to paddle all the way to the Blue Hole—to the disappearance of the Rio Camuy some three miles away.

We marked our maps: 1200 feet, 1500 feet—still the passage stretched ahead. The gravel carried into the boats by our repeated portages started to grind our knees, and it was a relief when our boats finally ran aground in shallow water at the entrance of a large chamber.

José and Vic were ahead, walking on a broad sand bar.

When John and I reached them Vic observed, "The river comes into the room from under that arch," pointing across the river to a low opening twenty feet wide and three feet high. "This must be the terminal pool and I guess only a side passage from the main cave."

<

Terry Tarkington and Jim Storey (*left*) pulling their boat through a shallow section of the river passage to reach deeper water (*right*). *Roy Davis*

Echo Hall and its weird formations. *Roy Davis*

Vic was probably right, and we decided to explore the dry passage instead and come back for the boats if we discovered the river again.

The sound of the water died behind us as we entered the silence of a corridor, actually a room, sixty feet high and fifty-five feet wide. While all of us were experienced cave explorers and knew the beauties to be seen underground, we were awed by this room, which for eons had remained unvisited until this moment. We carefully walked through a forest of stalagmites and beautiful white and onyx-colored formations. I was fascinated by the floor, which was completely covered with mud stalagmites—all untrod. On every side were weird-shaped formations. One moundlike stalagmite was distorted by the splattering of the water that dripped from a great height, causing the fantastic bulges and draperies of stone.

Each of us seemed to withdraw into himself. We walked silently through the room, enjoying the private thoughts that come with a profound emotional experience. The mapping was forgotten as we probed the black room with our flashlights to reveal these creations of the ages hidden beneath the earth.

Vic, who had gone on ahead, wrote in the log about the next room:

> The floor was plain mud, except for a single small but strikingly white stalagmite growing in the center. It stood out like a blob of whipping cream in a pot of hot chocolate.

But the passage that led from this dry room was richly decorated with flowstone, stalagmites thirty-five feet high, soda straws, cave pearls, and broomsticks—all secondary cave formations. For five hundred feet we walked through this delightful underground garden of cave formations until we came to a steep mud slope—the passage continuing ahead in the blackness. This beckoning entrance called us to explore farther, but we decided to leave some of the privilege of discovery to the second team, so we reluctantly turned back.

Remembering at least one of our missions, we placed a rock cairn in the passage as a station point and began to survey our way back to the river.

It was time for supper when we got back, and we gathered on the shore to eat our rations. As we talked, we became conscious of an odd echo, so for a few minutes we shouted and sang, while it accompanied us throughout the room. The peculiar acoustics permitted as much as a seven-second reverberation of certain tones.

We finished our vocal exercises and recorded the obvious name for the chamber, the Hall of Echoes. As we rose to leave, we noticed for the first time a number of bats swooping down to the water for a drink and flying low around our lights. We knew it must be getting dark outside, and that therefore they were getting ready to exit—but where?

A few flew into the arched opening over the river entrance, so we believed there must be an exit that way. Our belief was shattered after we counted those that returned and found they nearly matched the numbers that had left.

Returning to the boats, we started back downstream, dodging bats for a few minutes until they disappeared toward an unknown destination—another mystery to add to the others of the Rio Camuy.

Now that we were going with the current, we floated gently downstream, with hardly any effort necessary to make headway. A few pushes on the wall helped us keep in the middle of the stream.

Arriving at the Natural Bridge again, we decided to leave the boats and to swim out. This would leave boats for subsequent parties.

We waded most of the way toward the Big Room (the water became completely opaque because of the mud we stirred up as we sloshed along). I was leading the group when I stepped into a hole, and dropped into water up to my ears. Sputtering and gasping for air, I inflated my life jacket by pulling the CO_2 cylinder. It allowed me to bob along like a cork and float downstream to shallower water. From here on we all endured the inconvenience of inflated life jackets as we alternately waded and floated downstream.

When we splashed ashore at the foot of the Espiral entrance and looked up to where the opening to the sky should be, it looked like the rest of the cave—black. Night had fallen and, through we knew that this was the way out, we wondered how many other passages up the entranceway might be leading us astray in the darkness.

We picked our way upward—where we had seen Joe Lawrence climb hours before—and approached a seemingly impassable overhang. From this precipice dangled a wire ladder Team II had left for us. Unfortunately there was no safety rope visible. The ladder hung free for about thirty feet. We wondered how much ladder Joe had used. We suspected that it was two hundred feet to the entrance. Could the twenty feet be the beginning of a two-hundred-foot climb?

We checked our packs and found a fifty-foot rope and speculated that this might be long enough to use as a belay if we could go up in stages, positioning the party on ledges if necessary.

Roy Davis, the expedition rope man, was a mile away nursing a broken toe. And although none of the team would have hesitated to make the climb, I could not ask anyone to do it without a safety rope, so I volunteered.

I wound all fifty feet around my waist so that it would not

interfere with climbing. José held the bottom rung of the ladder taut, and I started up. Vic and John flattened themselves against the wall to avoid any rocks that might be dislodged as I climbed. It was easy going when the bottom was held tight, but when I reached the overhang José released his grip on the ladder to permit me to twist it off the wall so that I could get my fingers under the 3/8-inch aluminum rungs and pull myself over the edge. Raising myself to the level of the overhang, I set one shoulder against the flowstone and lurched over. My headlamp indicated a smooth slope ahead, about seventy degrees off vertical, and the wire ladder leading upward to a crevice, where it seemed to be secured. I scrambled up the steep slope and tumbled into the crevice, nearly bumping the iron bar that held the ladder. Next to it, neatly coiled, was a safety rope. As I suspected, everything had been carefully prepared. There was an additional rope—evidently the belay for the safety man—continuing up the crevice into the darkness and out. I tied a sufficient length of rope around myself as a belay, and called out below that I was off the ladder. The belay was tossed over the edge and the others ascended quickly to the surface.

Though the whole sky seemed lighted with stars, it was a moonless night. However, our eyes having been adapted to the cave, we had no difficulty picking out landmarks against the horizon of hills. We started our trek back without delay and we were soon in sight of the camp, where the glow of the gas lamps gave a pumpkinlike appearance to the open windows. We called as we drew near and in a minute everyone crowded around us to hear the news.

Team II was eager to continue the exploration, and the next morning Joe Lawrence, Jim Storey, Terry Tarkington, Al Mueller, and Dave Boyer (who went along to see what photographs he would plan for his subsequent coverage) went in. Dave had been introduced to caving only a few months before when he was on an assignment to photograph some of America's commercial caves for the National Geographic Society. It was a difficult assignment this time, for the Rio Camuy would have none of the conveniences that electrically lighted show caves have to offer. It was Team II's job to survey from the

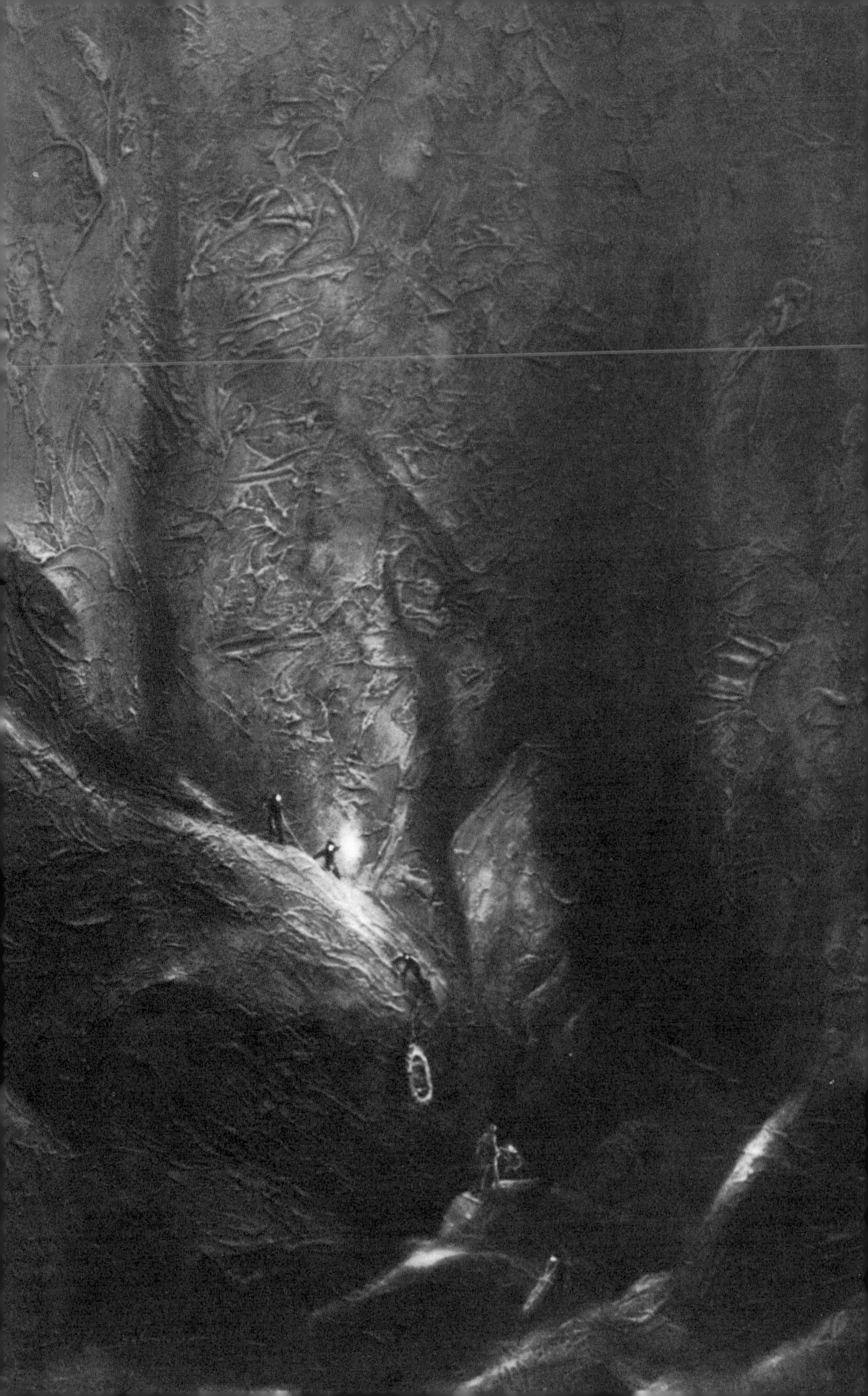

<
Coming down Espiral entrance.
Painting by John Schoenherr

A team member descending.
Roy Davis

Big Room to the Natural Bridge (our latest preliminary sketch was only for the information of exploring parties), installing station points that we could tie into when we made a more detailed study of the cave later. They were to continue from where we left off, past the Hall of Echoes.

They entered via Espiral Sink, taking with them four boats. They planned to leave a boat at strategic points to avoid portaging for exploring and working parties that would follow. Unfortunately, these old boats that John Spence had so carefully checked and patched would not stand up against the rigors of the cave. Two of the four ruptured and had to be abandoned before the end of the day, so not much time was saved. And the survey took considerable time, so, at the end of fourteen hours, they turned back after having reached the Hall of Echoes.

The next day's team continued with Terry and Jim, but replaced Joe, Al, and Dave with José and Vic. This lightly burdened and energetic crew pushed on to the Hall in three hours. There they had the choice of finding a route to the river, which appeared from a low-arched tunnel in the wall, or following the dry passage. They decided to attempt the river first and paddled under the arch upstream, about one hundred feet, to the terminal pool, pointed out earlier by Vic, and siphon (a point where water disappears beneath a wall); the walls of the pool extended straight down into the deep water. The only continuation appeared to be over a saddle on a flowstone mound above the pool, which seemed to lead to another room ahead. Terry

Terry Tarkington and a statuelike formation in the Hall of the White Maidens. *Roy Davis*

made the climb—a tricky one, as he had to start from the boat. He told us later:

> I attempted to climb the formation and was up about six or eight feet above the water when I slipped on the muddy handholds and footholds and slid back down into the water. When I hit the water the rubber boat was right by me and I grabbed it and only went up to my shoulders, not even putting my light out. My first thought as I found myself falling was how nice it would be to be in that clear blue-green water.

The second attempt, by Jim, was successful and so, with a hand line and belay, Terry and Jim went ahead another thirty feet, where they were stopped by a second siphon and an impossible climb without expansion bolts and special equipment.

Abandoning the water route, the team returned to Echo Hall and started in the dry passage, exploring side passages and small leads. Continuing beyond our brief visit several days before, they discovered a large room and named it the Hall of the White Maidens. This broad-sloped chamber was floored with breakdown and dotted with white formations resembling statues.

Sketches were made and survey data taken, at which time we named it the West Tributary, and finally the team started out for the trip back to camp. One of the boats had to be pumped up, as the rough treatment of the previous days began to take its toll on the fabric; small holes had begun to appear in practically all the boats after the first few days.

In the large room where Team I had discovered its echo quality, the party paused to eat. While Vic was entertaining them with several after-dinner arias, the rest of us back at camp were growing concerned. The long dry spell had broken suddenly, and for several hours a heavy rain fell steadily, drenching everything at camp not under cover. It had filled the nearly dry cistern to overflowing, and there was over an inch of rain accumulated in an empty paint bucket nearby.

Joe Lawrence and I decided to check the river and inform the team in the cave of the storm. At just about the time that Vic had completed his duet with himself, we started into the cave. The river was unchanged, and our high-water gauge showed no rise. We decided to go upstream anyway to see if we could help

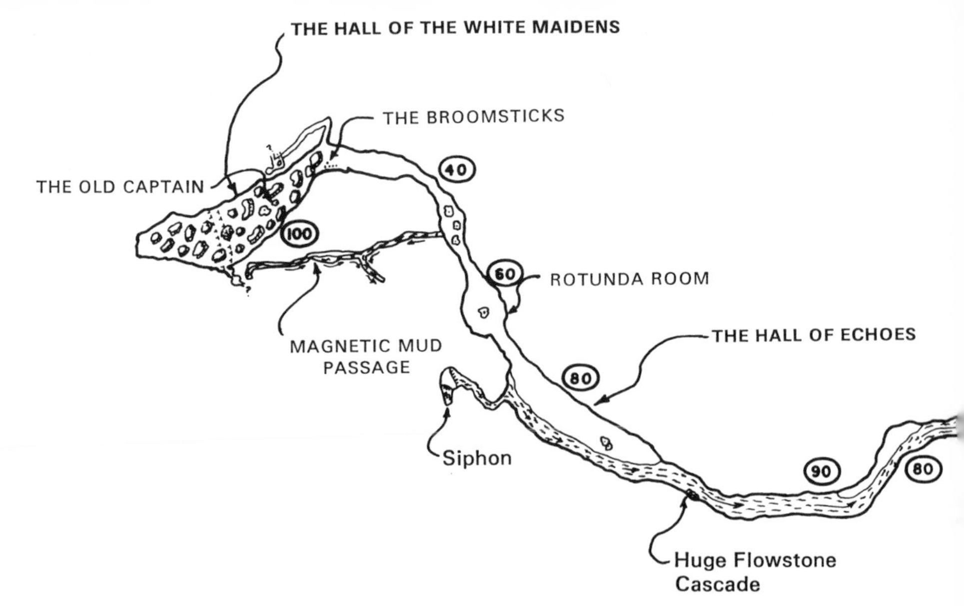

portage the boats in the Big Room, for the exploring party had been in the cave fourteen hours and would obviously be tired.

Our concern for the safety of the team was dispelled when we saw their lights across the Big Room, and the hike back to camp was accompanied by the enthusiastic reports of their findings.

The next day was clear and fair, and no evidence remained of the past evening's storm. We found it necessary to take this day to plot out our maps, put data together, and generally reorganize our forces for future exploration. But the photographic team, anxious to cover some of the area we had discovered, headed for the Tres Pueblos sinkhole to take some activity shots of Brother Nicholas and John Thrailkill.

Dave Boyer and Rick Wiker, the National Geographic Society photographers, had already stored some equipment in the cave, and they proceeded to set their "traps" to snare unwary cave explorers as they went about their work. To be caught in this snare meant serving a penance of being a model for several hours and helping shift photographic equipment about.

Vic and Terry went into the cave in the late afternoon to check the water gauge and walked directly into the area where the photographers were working. The two victims were conscripted for a picture at a spot across a pool and halfway up a waterfall. As Dave adjusted his camera, Vic, an avid conservationist, noticed that the pool was covered with flashbulbs and

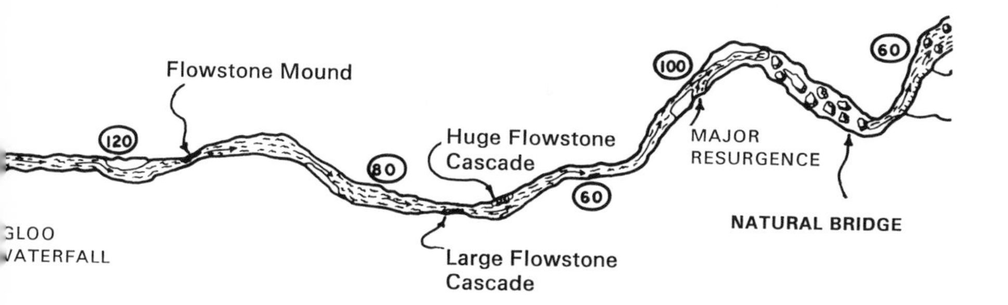

cartons. He was about to admonish the photographers for littering when he noticed that the bulbs were unused. And at the same moment the paddles from one of the boats disappeared into the swirling rapids.

"The river is rising!" Vic shouted. Terry, who had seen the paddles being swept away, had jumped into the water after them. Later, he explained:

> I swam across the first pool to the opposite wall, hanging on with my fingertips, which were badly cut by the razor-sharp edge of the rock. I could not hang onto the wall because the violent current tore me away from the handholds and I fell back into the raging water. Swimming with all my power to a rock, I pulled myself out, with the current still trying to pull me away from the rock and suck me back into the rapids of the main stream.

The team swiftly began to move all the equipment to higher ground. Vic remembered that the boat downstream was only lightly tied, and he dashed up the rough upper trail over the mountainous breakdown in a short cut to the river's edge. As he scrambled down to the water, the boat was tugging against the lines looped over partially submerged rocks. When he grabbed the line to pull the boat ashore, the paddles, which were in the end of the boat, slipped overboard and were swept away downstream. Vic shouldered the boat and climbed up to the

top of the mountain of jumbled rocks where the entire group was quickly assembling all the equipment into a pile.

The water was now five feet above normal, the once placid entrance pool was streaked with foam, and ugly swallets could be seen along the rocky edges of the river.

A hurried council determined that they should try to get out of the cave, but a hasty check of the equipment showed that there were no paddles; and another inspection of the watermark showed that the flood did not seem to be rising but had crested. This changed the feeling of urgency about leaving the cave, and it was decided to wait until the water receded to a point where it would be safe to drift out using only hands and poles for paddles.

The six men prepared to make the wait as comfortable as possible. And they took inventory of the food, carbide, batteries, and gasoline and found there was no need for alarm. The tension eased, and as the group relaxed, someone observed an apropos motto printed on one of the rubber boats: "Safe as the Ark." This led to the speculation about sending out a bat for a branch and the dismal thought of spending forty days and nights in their predicament. The mound of rocks was duly christened Mount Ararat, and the group began to exhaust their combined knowledge of the biblical story of the deluge as they waited for the water to go down.

A periodic check was made of the watermark. After the initial crest of five feet, the water receded gradually until four o'clock in the morning, when the group decided it was low enough to float out of the entrance without danger.

Back at camp, I had been sleeping fitfully. I was concerned about the photographic crew, who had planned to be back by midnight. I lay in my sleeping bag dozing and periodically looking at the luminous dial on my watch—when I realized it was 5:00 A.M. and we had received no word. I sat upright, searched for my boots, and picked my way over the sleeping bodies of the rest of the group. It was still dark as I went out the back door and over to the edge of the ravine where I would look toward the Tres Pueblos Sink. There I was delighted to see a little trail of bobbing lights. I went back and woke up Jeff Poxon, and, by

<
Flooding is sudden. *James Storey*

Left to right: Brother Nicholas, Rick Wiker, and John Spence in the laboratory corner of the casita. *Roy Davis*

the time the team arrived, water was boiling for a spaghetti and meatball supper they had missed the night before. It was nearly daylight when they wearily climbed into their sleeping bags.

Our plans were now set back a day. We had hoped to explore the route from the Empalme to the Tres Pueblos, but the flooding of the cave made us decide to rearrange our schedule. It was necessary to let the crew that had been trapped underground take a day to rest up. Photographic coverage of the new discoveries would have to be made on Friday, our last full day, or not at all. Roy Davis was recovering well from his fractured toe and was making dissatisfied noises about having to be in camp all day. He wanted to get in the cave. Finally, José put a Band-Aid on the toe and pronounced him cured.

We held council to see how we could most productively use the remaining time of the expedition. In reviewing the work to date, we were pleased that we had doubled the known extent of the passages; Brother Nicholas had found eight new animal species and one new genus; John Thrailkill had surveyed the area and talked with the local geologists from the United States Geological Survey and now had enough field data to prepare a report on the cave; and we had the cave fully rigged for work.

Only the photographic segment needed more coverage. This was not a reflection on the fine work Dave and Rick were doing; the unfortunate delay had been caused by high water. Consequently, we had no choice now but to concentrate on producing some pictures if we were to prepare a complete report for the Puerto Rican government and for our sponsors, The Explorers Club and the National Geographic Society.

We wanted to catch on film some of the scenes only a few of us had been able to see during the exploration. A six-man team was selected: Terry Tarkington (for the second time) and Jim Storey would be models; Roy Davis and Al Mueller would be photographers; and Vic Schmidt and Joe Lawrence would assist. Their objective was the Hall of the White Maidens, from which they would shoot just for the record all the way back to the entrance.

The rest of us would help Dave Boyer and Rick Wiker complete the work they had started in the Tres Pueblos area, where all their lighting equipment was still atop Mount Ararat.

Joe Lawrence wrote in the public log:

> February 14, 1964. Friday. This day I was scheduled to lead a six-man photographic party to the rear of the cave [the Hall of the White Maidens]. I awoke apprehensive about the trip. The underground course of the Rio Camuy is the most frightening cave I have ever explored. Floyd Collins' Crystal Cave is very fatiguing and easy to get lost in (I have done it); Clover Hollow Cave in Giles County, Virginia, has several spectacular and hair-raising drops in excess of 100 feet; but both Crystal and Clover Hollow are static. The river makes the Rio Camuy Caves dynamic. There can be sudden changes in the water level; swift currents tend to upset one's balance; potholes, boulders, and logs on the bottom are hidden from view by the water. I reflected on my accident of two years ago and I resolved to exercise extreme caution.

Joe's party left camp at 8:40 A.M. for the Espiral entrance. They took two boats that had been repaired at camp, but they soon discovered that some of the patches would not hold, and these caused problems all the way to Natural Bridge. Apparently rats had been night visitors in the cave (though we never saw one) and had chewed holes in the boats.

By 2:15 P.M. they were in the Echo Hall, where they started to take pictures. All afternoon they took photos of this room and of the Hall of the White Maidens, using up three rolls of film. The peculiar qualities of the Echo Room fascinated the party—the explosions of flash powder producing seven distinct echoes before disappearing.

Joe's log continued:

> As we moved downstream from the Echo Room we photographed portages and water passage. We attempted two flash powder shots, one of which was unsuccessful because of motion between flashes.
>
> Two two-year-old boat began to leak and had to be pumped up several times. Three different materials (rubber cement, Epoxy, and Iron Bound) had been used in patching it. All three failed.
>
> Before reaching Natural Bridge we discontinued taking pictures because of the boat difficulties and human fatigue.

This ended the picture-taking. Now it was the struggle back to the entrance. They arrived back at camp at 1:00 A.M., a very tired crew.

The major objectives of the expedition had been accomplished. The next day we packed, secured our house, and left for San Juan—each with the satisfaction that he had coordinated and cooperated in excellent fashion.

We departed Puerto Rico feeling that, while only begun, our work in this huge underground system was a giant step toward unraveling an unknown natural resource—the mysteries of the underground Camuy.

chapter V

Our explorations at the Rio Camuy were well publicized among the cavers of the United States. But it was also known to many of our friends, some who had been on expeditions, who expressed an interest in taking a "visitor's" trip through the cave. So in July of 1964 we were again at the little house, this time with our daughter Susan, Bill and Merle Stephenson, and Ackie and Betty Loyd.

Although Susan was only twelve years old, she was an experienced caver. She had entered her first cave at the age of five months on Jeannie's back in a papoose board, and had been in several hundred caves with the family through the years. I felt no concern about her going into the cave.

Bill Stephenson founded the National Speleological Society in 1941, and served on its board of directors for twenty-five years. He is large, agile, and fearless (but aware of the dangers and pitfalls of any cave), and I knew it would be a treat for me to show him the Camuy cave.

Ackie and Betty Loyd, experienced cavers from Virginia, had explored caves in West Virginia with us and had also been with us on a trip to Guatemala.

When we checked the boats (we had left them in our headquarters after the February expedition), we could find only two that appeared to be in good enough condition to make the cave traverse: so Merle, Betty, and Jeannie therefore volunteered to stay ashore, and Bill, Ackie, Susan, and I would go in through the Tres Pueblos entrance and on to the Big Room. We planned to stay only a few hours and then return.

We were pleased to discover that the river appeared nearly normal. It was slightly over the February level, but nothing to concern us. At the bottom of the sink we checked our life jackets and extra lights and prepared to launch—for what was to be an unexpected adventure. The following is Sue's account:

> The constant sound of the coffee-colored water pounding over the rocks at the entrance made it difficult to hear Dad's instructions. We paddled from the green-filtered sunlight into the semi-darkness of the first chamber. Soon we were out of the sight of light and paddling hard against the current. At a landing we had to portage, pushing the rubber raft through a tight side passage to a waterfall, where we stopped.
>
> The food had been left behind, so Dad went back to retrieve our lunch. While I tended my balky carbide lamp, the other two men went exploring. I was left alone, and was leaning against a telephone-pole-sized log that had been swept in by a previous flood. By the lamp's dim spotlight I noticed movement on the floor and saw a frighteningly large crab and several shiny cockroaches that scurried about when my light shown full upon them. I wished the rest of the group would return.
>
> We started again, paddling up a water-filled subway-tunnel-type passage. I was intrigued by the water-worn scallop patterns of the walls.
>
> At the Big Room we left the boats and, after climbing up to the highest point, Dad lighted magnesium ribbon for us to see how large the room really was.
>
> The blue after-image of the burning tape strained my eyes. I was hungry, wet and a bit uneasy.

"Let's eat so we can get out of here," said Mr. Stephenson.

Dad began to untie the lunch knapsack, but before we could eat any of the food we heard the sound of the river change. It was suddenly louder, and seemed to be traveling across the room. Dad scooped up the sack and headed down the slope. Mr. Loyd sensed his action and followed. Mr. Stephenson and I picked up the remaining things and quickly clambered down to the river level.

The water was rising and the boats were adrift—tugging at the lines that were now tied under water. Dad caught the line of our boat, but Mr. Loyd had to jump into the water to retrieve the end of the rope that was just slithering over the wet rocks as we arrived. Then Mr. Loyd jumped into the front boat and Mr. Stephenson tried to get into the back, but he slipped and splashed down into the water. He grabbed for the boat, but the current carried him to the main stream of the river. I saw the boat with one man inside and one man in the water swirling downstream in the powerful current.

Dad hesitated only a few seconds; then we quickly jumped in our boat and paddled after them, which was like trying to peddle down a steep hill on a one-speed bicycle. The walls flew by and the scallop-wall pattern was nothing but a gray blur. The other boat had disappeared around the bend; and the river was now an angry, churning white-water sluice. We swept around the bend and saw the other boat hugging the right wall. Mr. Stephenson had caught hold of a projection with one hand and Mr. Loyd's boat with the other as we shot toward them. The sound of the river increased to a roar, and we were approaching the waterfall we had passed on our way in.

"Paddle hard to the right!" cried Dad, and I paddled as hard as I could as we swept past Mr. Loyd. He caught Dad's paddle and we swung against the wall; I grabbed a rock and we stopped.

Mr. Stephenson climbed out of the water and all of us then crawled along a narrow ledge, tugging the boats so we could get above the waterfall. We dragged the boats out of the water, and huddled together to wait for the water to subside.

I had gone up first and was at the end of the shelf overlooking the waterfall. I was tired, hungry and frightened. Mr. Stephenson, next to me with his wet, cold coveralls and life jacket, was not comforting. I crouched near the wall, with my lamp, nearly against the rock. A small soda straw stalactite was right in front of my eyes, and to pass the time, I counted the drops of water as they fell relentlessly, drop by drop. I counted over a hundred when Dad said we were going to move on.

Mr. Loyd and Dad had removed the ropes from the boats and tied them into one long line. With this rope, each of us climbed down to the water level past the waterfall, where we launched the boats again into the boiling pool just downstream of the cascade. Mr. Loyd's boat was sent across the pool tied to the rope; then I went across with a rope tied at both ends. This was the landing place where I had met the crabs and cockroaches. I looked for them while I waited for Mr. Stephenson and Dad to get safely across the pool, but none were in view.

The water had not risen any farther. The climb over the mountain called Mount Ararat meant more pushing and pulling of the boats. We could see the green soft light of the Tres Pueblos Sink ahead. The brown water was five feet above the stage that we had seen it only a few hours before. It was now capped with little white wavelets. The green moss and twisted stalactites blended with the brown and black rocks. It was hard to imagine that the beautiful water could have changed from a peaceful river to an angry torrent in only a few minutes. We launched the boats and paddled hard to escape the rapids just outside the entrance. As we staggered ashore, I felt as if we had battled with nature and won.

Susan was not alone in being grateful to make an exit from the cave. I had been more concerned on this trip than on any other. The responsibility of the others fell heavily on me, and because of the complete trust Susan showed in me, it was all the more important that there be no mishap. The cave had held my respect before, but now I was absolutely convinced that the Rio Camuy could not be trusted to be the benign or provident stream it appeared to be in dry season. From here on I would keep up my guard and be more insistent than ever that all safety precautions be observed.

At home again in the United States, we prepared our report of the previous expedition for the National Geographic Society's *Research Reports, 1963 Projects,* and provided all the information to the Puerto Rican government. We thought that surely now they would be excited about the potential of this beautiful, natural area. But after we received a response that reflected interest in the work that had been done, nothing happened.

Eighteen months went by, and just when we began to

despair that we would accomplish anything, an event occurred that started things going again.

It was a party, not a big one, just an afternoon get-together, but significant in the story of the Rio Camuy. It came about as follows:

In the summer of 1965, we decided to take a family vacation to our little house in Puerto Rico. Included were Jeannie, our daughters, Susan and Wendy, my mother, and I. Mother, who was in her 70's and had never been to the island before, was interested to see what we talked about so much.

Soon after we landed, we settled ourselves in our headquarters house, which now boasted gas lights, a refrigerator, and sleeping cots. But time had taken its toll, so the girls scrubbed and cleaned until it looked very presentable. For recreation, we rented a horse from Sonny Rodriguez, and that made our preteen daughters ecstatic. Unfortunately, the terrain was so rugged throughout the twenty-two acres that there was hardly a level place to ride. Undaunted, the girls contented themselves with grooming his mane until it glistened, and braiding ribbons into it.

Jeannie wandered around the property with my mother, showing her the begonias growing wild between the limestone rocks near the house and the wild orchids on the trees by the Tres Pueblos Sink. It was an idyllic time, one of the first trips we made without a specific project to keep us busy. The weather was hot, but the nights were cool.

Of course, I could not let a trip to the island go by without contacting members of the government, and soon I had arranged to present an illustrated talk for several officials in San Juan. It was well received, and I invited everyone present to visit the cave area on the following Sunday.

The arrangements were for them to meet at the intersection of Routes 129 and 455 (right over the Empalme entrance) and then the group would head for the little house. I waited for them by the road as their cars appeared, two or three at a time, soon creating a traffic jam on the narrow road. I arranged for them to park in the yard of a small store, and we walked back to the house. When we were all assembled I was a little overwhelmed to see that twenty-four members of the Administration had appeared. The group had been contacted by Ramon Garcia Santiago, chairman of the Planning Board. Included were Felix Mejias, director of the Land Administration, Ricardo Alegria of the Department of Culture, members of the Park Commission, senators, and other officials.

We all stood in the front yard of the casita as I introduced the family. Then Jeannie, the girls, and I led the way down the trail with the whole group.

Not everyone was dressed for a hike in the country, certainly no one for a trip through a cave. But everyone was eager to go as we went down the ravine and into the orange grove.

We went into the dry, upper entrance of the Empalme Cave, and everyone seemed impressed, although a number of highly polished shoes were now streaked with cave mud. We chatted and huffed and puffed back up the steep trail to the house.

Someone had thrown open the green-stained glass windows to provide a perfect view of the karst hills, and in a moment our casita was bursting with people, and Jeannie was offering hors d'oeuvres and cool drinks she had prepared. That was the party and the turning point.

It was a nostalgic experience for many of the men. They were reminded of earlier years when they had visited similar summer homes. The walk through the beautiful rain forest in the ravine was an eloquent reminder of less hectic times and certainly a far different world from the paneled offices and pressures of the administrative world to which they had now become accustomed.

Ramon Garcia Santiago, the chairman of the Planning Board, was particularly enthusiastic. I spoke with him at length of our hopes and plans for the development of the area and caves. Apparently it was appealing to him, for he wrote to me later in the United States:

"The visit to the cave was a very pleasing experience to all of us. It's like rediscovering a spot of beauty. We were impressed with the work done so far by you and only hope that it might be completed on your next visit."

At that moment a plan for another expedition was being born. This time we would do what had never before been done on such a scale: create a blueprint specifically for the development of a virgin cave, using the best specialists we could find.

This was a challenge I leaped at—an opportunity peculiarly suited to my interest. I had no practical experience in cave development but I knew almost everyone in the United States who had successfully developed a cave.

The interest shown by Señor Santiago, and Felix Mejias as well, was the key, and I lost no time in following it up.

I prepared an estimate for the expenses of fielding such an expedition, including the costs of printing a report in the *Bulletin* of the *National Speleological Society* and sent it to Señor Mejias. I was delighted to receive a letter by return mail, stating in part:

"Hereby the Land Administration of Puerto Rico commits itself to pay a maximum of $3,000 for the study and its publication in the Society's *Bulletin*."

The date for the new expedition was set for February 3–13, 1966, and on October 23, 1965, the board of governors of the National Speleological Society approved it as an official expedition. We now had less than ninety days to coordinate and field a team that would accomplish what appeared to be an imposing task.

Some of the preliminary work had been done by Brother Nicholas, who had been continuing work in the ecological study of the cave and surrounding area through the participation of La Salle College in Philadelphia. He had planned another trip over the Christmas holidays, but I convinced him that he should join us, thereby postponing his trip until February. This gave us the nucleus of our scientific personnel. Things moved rapidly, and in a few weeks I had commitments from those who had previously worked at the Rio Camuy—stalwarts who provided the backbone of the working team: José Limeres agreed to go; Al Mueller, as an electrical engineer, would study the cave from an engineering point of view; Jim Storey, as a civil engineer, would consider the mechanical problems in developing the cave—in addition to the role he usually played in safety and rope work; John Spence would again coordinate our needs for mechanical equipment; he was also the treasurer for the group; Jeannie would again be indispensable in providing solutions to the thousands of problems that would arise from beginning to end, in addition to putting out the *Bulletin;* Roy Davis on this trip would be photographer, explorer, and cave-lighting consultant; he had designed and installed lighting for more than twenty commercial caves in the United States.

Selecting experts to evaluate the cave as an overall commercial venture was more difficult. We needed someone to determine the economic possibilities.

Jack Herschend, president of Silver Dollar City and Marvel Cave in Missouri, was the logical choice. The City continues to attract millions of people. Jack was also the first president of the National Caves Association. However, in his modesty, he describes his position on our team as "to tell them where to put the cash register."

Jack Burch, of Natural Bridge Cave in Texas, came to mind for developing the cave trails. He had participated in the development of Texas's Sonora Caverns, one of the most remarkable show caves in the country, and later helped discover and develop Natural Bridge Cave. Jack's trail work was impressive for its sensitivity. However, to convey a tourist through a cave is a matter of judicious vandalism and, to a man as discerning as Jack, such a task must always have been painful. But the results he had obtained in maintaining the natural beauty of the above-mentioned caves were outstanding.

We had need for additional expertise. On past expeditions we had always tried to capture the type and magnitude of a cave by photography and mapping. But the Rio Camuy particularly is almost impossible to photograph because of the tremendous size of its rooms. Here was an opportunity to carry out an idea that had always intrigued me: taking along an artist to give us a full perspective. I lost no time in contacting John Schoenherr, a professional illustrator and an experienced spelunker. Since he was a free-lance artist and his time was his own, he was delighted to get away to Puerto Rico for a couple of weeks to sketch one of his favorite subjects.

Each of the seasoned Rio Camuy investigators was now two years older, and the rigors of the cave were well known to all of us. So we were faced with the need again for a young, strong, able rope man. I put in a call to the Texas Speleological group for a man to do both rope work and surveying. They selected Orion Knox of Austin. We were to receive a bonus in Orion, as he was also an architect and, later, was able to provide the drafting and design for the proposed surface development.

The last, and very important, space to be filled was that of cook. Brother Nicholas suggested Carol Lochner of Pearl River, New York. Carol was also a nurse, and we knew that between her and Jeannie and John Spence our creature comforts would be provided for.

Plans were finally complete; tickets and itineraries were drawn, and the heavy equipment had been sent ahead.

Since we were spread all over the United States, the meeting place for the team was San Juan Airport, at the Avis Rent-a-Car booth, at noon, February 3, 1966.

Once again our casita above the Rio Camuy was bursting with people. John Spence was now well acquainted with the vagaries of the equipment and had found methods of supplying water and shoring up the sagging floor. The kitchen had been modernized with a two-burner propane stove, and an ice supply was located for the defunct refrigerator now turned icebox.

Most of the crew had been on the 1962 expedition, so on arrival they immediately began to pitch tents and set up camp. Only Brother Nicholas was missing, and he would be delayed a few days because of his schoolwork. We had the manpower now to set up an outdoor shower alongside a small cliff in the back of the house; it featured a magnificent cross-country view and fully equipped built-in soap dishes provided by the little niches in the limestone ledge. The crew on this trip felt very civilized and hardly handicapped by the living accommodations. Of course, the most important feature of the house was our incredible "re-creation room" four hundred feet below.

But this time, exploring the depths would have a different purpose: to look at it through the eyes of the experts who were here to prepare a practical and efficient way to develop the area we had indicated for tourists.

We spread out maps and photos and began to brief the new members.

Pure exploration was not dead, however, as we had some unfinished business to take care of. On our last trip we had never been able to make the traverse from the Empalme entrance to Tres Pueblos. On the day we had scheduled it, the group had been trapped in the cave by the flood. Joe Lawrence, who still wanted to make the traverse but was unable to join us on this trip, was replaced by Al Mueller as leader of the team.

We knew the distance was about a half mile as the crow flies, but had no idea how far it might be underground. Al Mueller, José Limeres, Roy Davis, and our new team member, Orion Knox, would make the attempt.

In the meantime, Jim Storey would go with John Spence and rig ladders and safety ropes for the teams to use as they went in and out of the Espiral entrance.

Jack Herschend, Jack Burch, John Schoenherr, and I would make a reconnaissance trip into the "tourist" section from Tres Pueblos to the Natural Bridge.

Jeannie and Carol had mastered the equipment in the house and had set it up for easiest use. We would have buffet-style meals, but sit at a common table so that everyone could discuss each day's plans and developments. At other times, the table would be used for group meetings.

By ten the next morning all the teams were in the cave, each starting from a different place: Al Mueller at Empalme, Jim Storey at Espiral, and the rest of us at Tres Pueblos.

For my group, it would be a shakedown trip, to let these men see the cave to determine the equipment they would use and areas they would work in during the rest of the week.

My trip was a delight. I was the only one who had been in the cave before, and it was a treat to show it to such an appreciative audience. We carried six-volt lanterns to permit us to probe the upper regions of the rooms and to look for high passages. I pointed out the evidence of high water—twigs and wood lodged in crevices in one place thirty-five feet above the present water level. Also, we probed the high walls for possible tourist routes.

At the Big Room I climbed to the highest point and lighted it with some magnesium ribbon. With the powerful electric torches we were able to take some survey triangulation sights on the ceiling and on the width of the room. The ceiling from the water was close to two hundred and fifty feet in one spot, and the width exceeded two hundred feet. The total length of the Big Room was nearly six hundred feet.

Both Jacks were discussing the few short, stumplike stalagmites on a steep slope nearby, mentioning that it was nothing too spectacular as a point of interest for tourists. They wondered if there might be another, more scenic route. Nor was the lower part of the room too suitable for a trail, as it was littered with huge blocks of breakdown and would necessitate bridging.

We returned to the river and proceeded upstream, scanning upper walls with our torches as we went. When Jack Herschend pointed out an upper level about forty feet above the water, we beached the boats and scrambled up the slippery wall to that section.

We were on a long, level, natural shelf fifty feet wide and forty feet above the river. This was virgin cave—the floor untrampled mud—and the wall rose one hundred feet to the ceiling. Jack Burch immediately saw the advantage of this natural trail, as we hurriedly walked along toward the Natural Bridge.

After a while we took a more leisurely pace as our lights began to pick up some beautiful stalagmites and rimstone pools that bordered the trail—its uniform elevation continuing almost to the Natural Bridge; both Jacks were busy visualizing a possible route that would show the scene to best advantage.

We arrived at the Natural Bridge, retraced our steps, and exited at the Espiral entrance, which Jim Storey had rigged.

Back at headquarters, about 6:00 P.M., we discovered Al and his party. They had been stopped by lack of equipment, but they were going to try again the next day.

After supper we held a council. Jack Herschend and Jack Burch were satisfied that they had seen ample cave to provide a most spectacular tourist trip. Now it would be a matter of determining how best to exhibit it.

One thing disturbed me greatly. I felt that we would have

a difficult time providing an accurate plan for a tourist route unless we had a more exact survey of the cave—one that would be coordinated with the surface so that the location of an elevator could be determined for use in transporting visitors in or out. While we had anticipated this problem and had brought surveying equipment capable of improving the accuracy of our maps, such a survey would still be difficult and very time-consuming.

I unrolled our surface map of the area and pointed out to Jack Herschend the underground route of the river we had traveled that day: the Tres Pueblos entrance, the Espiral entrance, the Big Room, and, finally, the Natural Bridge. "What we need is another natural entrance about here," I said, moving my finger in a circle over the Natural Bridge.

Jack looked at me incredulously and said kiddingly, "Sure, why not? That's a lot closer to the road, too!"

"Seriously," I continued, "it's worth a try to see if there is another opening somewhere upstream of the Espiral entrance. The possibility of a closure with a surface point for our survey would eliminate any error on our old map."

I'm not sure what Jack thought, but the next morning the two Jacks and I started up the road for the area I had pointed to on the map. We would need this closure to confirm that the cave was winging due west from Natural Bridge.

José Limeres that morning had gone back to the cave with Al Mueller, so we were without our translator. But we stopped at a little grocery nearby our destination and after a few moments I found that the owner, Philip, spoke excellent English. I asked him if there were any "blowing holes" on the property, and he said there were several on the hill beyond the house.

Jack Herschend gave me an odd look as we started up the hill, following the verbal directions Philip had given us.

The knoll behind the house (actually a small karst haystack) was more than a hundred feet high. It was smoothly rounded and the area was fenced to keep in Philip's several cows. Inside, it was easy to find the lone clump of trees that he said surrounded the hole. A single barbed wire fence prevented any cattle from falling into it. As we approached it, we were greeted with a blast of fetid, hot air that told us there was something dead down there. But neither could you miss the definite blowing action from the black opening, and it certainly looked promising.

We looked at our map and oriented ourselves with the landmarks around the house.

"We should be directly over the river," I said, "but we won't know for sure unless we drill a hole or unless that blow hole leads us to something."

We spent the rest of the day walking over the surface around the cave area, arriving back at the house just as Al and his party returned. Al, Jim Storey, Orion Knox, and José Limeres had made the traverse.

We listened to their vivid description of the cave beyond the waterfall (the one just upstream from the bottom of the Empalme sinkhole). Jim Storey and Orion had rigged the waterfall with a cable ladder only to find at the top that the falls were actually back to back with falls going the other way. It was apparent when they reached the top that the main river actually went under this wall-to-wall choke, or barrier, in the passageway. A second stream, about fifty feet from the floor in the upper reaches of the passageway, flowed both ways off the crown of the choke. Over the years this flow had deposited forty feet of calcite to fill the passage. It was necessary to rig both sides of the falls in order to continue.

They had left the waterfall rigged so it would now be easy to make the traverse from either direction.

Beyond the waterfall they found a large room more than two hundred feet high and full of bats. The droppings of these creatures made the room unpleasant and slippery, and they lost no time in traversing it. The group continued upstream to a long, sinuous water passage, which varied in height from sixty to one hundred feet—with only one blockage similar to the one they had previously passed.

From there they made an easy exit from Tres Pueblos Sink. At least half of the trip had required the use of the boats, as the water was usually more than six feet deep.

Their report cleared up any doubts about that section of the Rio Camuy and reconfirmed our earlier choice for a tourist route.

It was late evening now, and having been pleased with Al's

account, our attention turned back to the blow hole, which we named La Ventosa. Before we retired, we made plans for a group to go there the next day to see where it led.

In the morning I took Jack Herschend, Jack Burch, Roy Davis, and Orion Knox to Philip's tienda. It was my intention to leave them and return to the house, but I just had to stay. However, Philip was already at the hole with some friends.

As we approached the opening we were again greeted by the foul odor of the warm breeze.

"A dead dog, Señor," said Philip as Orion dropped gingerly into the hole. The rest followed, I along with them, as my curiosity pulled me on.

It was only a few feet to the floor of the first chamber, where the dog was conspicuously dead. We skirted the spot, trying to stay out of the draft that was now almost overpowering.

As I arrived, I saw the others looking down a pit at the lower end of the chamber. It looked as if we would need a ladder, but Jack Herschend took the end of a handline and, secured by Jack Burch, lowered himself to a level floor fifteen feet below. Looking down, I could see a low arch, through which Jack now disappeared. He soon called for us to follow, so I slid down the rope and joined him in a low room that dropped off into blackness.

"Listen," said Jack, and as we concentrated, we could hear the murmur of the river somewhere below. We tried to shine our lights in that direction but the beam did not reach bottom. This was obviously a job for the rope men, so Jack and I returned to the rest of the party. While a decent burial was prepared for the poor dog, Jack and I returned to camp to get Jim Storey and the climbing equipment.

The subsequent descent made with Jim Storey and Roy Davis is described by Orion:

> We got all the equipment down to the top of the big drop. It was sure eerie looking. We strung out our long rope down the drop; I hooked into my seat sling and got all my gear into the bag and over my shoulder. Then I started down. I dropped over three ledges about a hundred feet down, and then there was

> a free fall for the rest of the way. I landed in the middle of a large passage, signaled that I was on the bottom and took a look around. First I went north and after about one hundred and fifty feet I found myself over the river passage. I returned to the rope and called for Jim and Roy to come on down. Jack Burch stayed at the top.

Jim was next, sliding down the rope on his metal brake bar for a descent of about two hundred and thirty feet. His ride was more enjoyable because he could see the bottom lighted by Orion's lamp.

Roy followed and soon all three were gathered at the bottom of the rope. They set off toward the sound of the river.

Jim Storey recalls:

> We were now overlooking a steep mud bank with a platform below. I rigged the slope with a 75-foot piece of nylon rope and then proceeded down to what appeared to be a natural bridge which was high above the rushing water. We decided that we needed more rope so we cut another hundred feet off the spool in order to make the descent. We rigged Roy with his ascenders [metal climbing clamps] in case he landed in water over his head. Fortunately, the water was shallow enough for him to land safely, so we followed him to the bottom. We discovered we were in a known part of the cave [just upstream of where Joe Lawrence had his boulder accident four years before]. We were thrilled at connecting this new discovery, so by prusik and jumars climbed back up the rope to the perch over the river. Going up the mud slope was tricky and required the use of jumars to safely make it.

Then, while Jim started on the long, slow climb back up the hanging rope to where Jack was waiting, Roy and Orion took a look around. The passage they had landed in was dry and nearly level. They proceeded in a southwest direction for about a thousand feet and then, concerned that Jim and Jack might be wondering about them, they returned to the rope and tied in the equipment to be pulled up. Orion and then Roy followed. Jim's last entry in the log read: "What a climb! We were all muddy and exhausted."

There was jubilation in camp when they returned. The

A rope descent into La Ventosa.
Roy Davis

A ladder descent into La Ventosa.
Roy Davis

discovery of the new entrance permitted us to survey from the surface of La Ventosa to a station point near the Natural Bridge on our original survey, which Vic Schmidt and Terry Tarkington had made two years before. In spite of our difficulty in getting accurate station points in our boats, our original map was accurate within one hundred feet (less than a 3-percent error). This important discovery cut two days off the time we still needed for further survey.

Jack Herschend seemed to be the only one who didn't realize the sheer luck of the discovery. Apparently my earlier confidence that there had to be an entrance where we needed it had convincd him of its existence, and he now took it for granted.

With a good part of our work now done, we reviewed the fine job Al Mueller's team had done in making the traverse from the Empalme to Tres Pueblos entrance. We would have only to map that section, but this would be the first time we would enter the cave going downstream, with the current, instead of the safer paddle against it. That is, the two Jacks and Roy and I would reverse the route by entering at Tres Pueblos.

We had everything going for us. The two boats left at the entrance by Al's party were ready to go. His description of the cave showed no tricky places, and the waterfall at Empalme had been rigged.

The water level was normal, but just a few feet out of the sight of light the tunnel narrowed to a sluiceway with only six feet of headroom. The water ran swiftly through this constriction and, as each boat steered through the middle of the passage, there was a definite toboggan feeling as the boat picked up speed and undulated over the surging water. The passage ahead was unobstructed and straight, and the sights easy to read, so we floated nicely along. At about eight hundred feet downstream, we came to a pool, deep and still, but filled with bamboo and debris floating on the surface. We pushed our way through this mess and proceeded.

<
Landing after the descent. *Roy Davis*

When we reached the Bat Room we had to portage the boats. I went ahead with Jack Herschend to select a route while Roy and Jack Burch continued the survey. This two-hundred-foot-high room was more than a hundred feet wide, and the stream made an S-shaped sweep through a center channel on the level floor. It went over several low falls and then into what appeared to be deep water up ahead. I suggested to Jack Herschend that we try to run the river in one of the boats while Roy and Jack Burch continued surveying on shore. This appealed to him, as he is an expert canoeist and a dedicated Missouri river man.

We jumped into the boat and for a few minutes we enjoyed a thrilling ride between the boulders and through the sluices of the stream. We floated up to a point where we could see the rigged forty-foot waterfall flowing over a solid wall of beautifully sculptured flowstone, and then paddled ashore to wait for the others.

Roy and Jack Burch arrived and paused to admire it. On one side of the falls was an aluminum ladder, with safety rope, leaning out at about 70 degrees so as to keep it out of range of the hurtling water. The end of the ladder dangled in the water, so it was necessary to start our climb from the boats.

"It looks as if it's an impossible climb from this side," I said to Roy, who had been on the first trip to the top of the waterfall from the other side.

"No," said Roy, "There are plenty of handholds; but it would be difficult to find a place to start from the water."

Starting from the boats, though, we had no trouble with the ladder, and, as assured, there were plenty of handholds. But problems occurred from an unexpected quarter. I was to be the last man up; Roy was part way up; and Jack Herschend and Jack Burch were on top ready to haul up the boats. The first boat went up all right, but, as I began to climb the ladder, the second boat, now free, was sucked into the waterfall. By the time I could pull it back with the tow line, it had shipped about four hundred pounds of water. It was impossible to dump the water and I couldn't lift the boat because of my awkward position on the ladder. So I climbed down into a nearly submerged boat and

>

Al Mueller (*left*) and Orion Knox at the Empalme waterfall. *James Storey*

slowly paddled back to a nearby sandy beach. Here I was able to turn it over and drain out the water. At the ladder, this time I wound the stern rope to a stalagmite to one side of the waterfall before I got out of the boat, and we carefully hauled it clear.

Once over the falls it was an easy matter to gather all the rope, ladders, and equipment and make our Empalme entrance exit.

As we came up the trail to our headquarters, we could see that the front yard, usually a clutter of equipment and drying gear, was empty, and the clatter of pots being scraped in the kitchen made us think that we might have missed lunch. We got almost to the front yard before anyone noticed we were back.

José, Al Mueller, and Jack Schoenherr came out of the front door dressed in sports clothes, and Al said, "Come on! Hurry up. We're going swimming in Arecibo."

I had forgotten that we had decided that everyone would go to town that day for some swimming. We stood there looking forlorn in our muddy clothes while Jim Storey, carrying an ice carton, came out of the house and headed toward the highway.

We were sure that we had missed lunch when Jeannie came to the door with a plate of sandwiches.

"Here's something to eat while you change."

No one asked us what we had done, so we dutifully pulled off our soggy clothes and munched our sandwiches, feeling a little neglected. This feeling wore off very quickly when we sponged off in the water barrel and got into some clean clothes.

We even enjoyed the trip on the old Bayaney-Arecibo road in a microbus with ten people—a journey that has to be experienced to be appreciated. The sun-roof permitted three in the center to stand, which gave them an unobstructed view of the road ahead—for a few hundred yards at best, considering the 132 twists in a four-mile stretch. But with a red arch of flowering flamboyant branches overhead, we had the illusion of rushing down a winding tunnel.

Following the road that skirted Arecibo, the bus continued east across a bridge to the ocean road, heading for an area of the beach not too far from a sea cave known as La Cueva del Indio.

Because this area, like the rest of the northern coast of Puerto Rico, is exposed to the open ocean, no protecting headlands or reefs break the full force of the wind and waves. Only a few sheltered coves contain the broad, sweeping sand that one expects in the Caribbean. But there are some fine beaches, and the spot we selected was protected by tongues of black-pitted rock worn away by the constant dashing of the waves.

At high tide the waves flood over this low tidewater and fill a large circular pool. A splendid swimming area is left—about five or six feet deep, depending on the tides. The sun warmed the water, and it was delightful to swim only a hundred yards from the crashing surf that was throwing twenty-foot-high waves and showers of foam on the black rocks.

Everyone scattered about, while Jeannie and I walked along

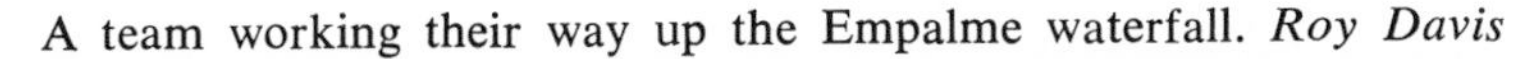

A team working their way up the Empalme waterfall. *Roy Davis*

the shore, wading in the shallow water and looking for shells. We stopped and tried to tease a little hermit crab out of his shell.

The sky began to cloud over, and the beautiful aqua color of the shallow pool turned blue-gray. The wind picked up and the white, fluffy clouds darkened. It looked as though it might rain, so we raced back to the microbus and drove off to the supermarket for supplies before continuing on to camp.

When we got back to the house, Brother Nicholas had arrived by *publico*, or public bus, from San Juan. We brought him up to date on all the discoveries, and it was getting to be a noisy party when Carol (as a complete surprise to us all) produced a cake decorated with candles. The celebration was for an anniversary—Jeannie and I had been married fifteen years. It could not have been a more pleasant end to a perfect day.

Half of our field-trip time was gone and it was now necessary to fill in the details of the different aspects each man was here to cover. With an outline agreed upon, our attitude underwent a subtle change. We now became engaged purely in professional expertise.

Jim Storey exchanged his caving hard hat for that of the civil engineer, hiking and planning for an entrance road to the cave.

Jack Burch pored over the maps and clambered up and down the sinkhole trails, mulling over the technical problems of a foot trail for the throngs of people who would one day follow us. He knew from experience the physical difficulties of transporting tons of concrete into a cave for walks, steps, bridges, supports, and so on.

Jack Herschend also reverted to his daily occupation. While the rest of us felt that we trod virtually uninhabited acreage, Jack conjured up a congregation of five to ten thousand people a day. He saw parking, transportation, sewage, and communications problems, and deliberated "where to put the cash register." He and I visited the tourist bureau in San Juan and talked with Señor Barasorda to learn the visitor flow to the island. We also

<
Downstream side of Empalme waterfall. *Russell Gurnee*

estimated the local flow potential and the bus capacity. From the Highway Department we obtained the plans for the proposed Arecibo-Lares-Mayagüez highway, which would someday pass near the cave.

Al Mueller checked out the potential power needs for lights, elevators, trams, and pumps.

Roy Davis approached the project as one of a series of similar challenges he had faced in providing dramatic lighting for caves all over the United States. He knew from experience the enormous amount of light necessary to show some of the huge rooms below. He also knew the value of the "pools of darkness" needed to provide the mystery and drama so important in the presentation of this natural wonder.

Brother Nicholas had never deviated from his profession. He had been studying the life of the cave for several years, and his job was one of haste. He must continue to investigate the cave in its pristine state before the plans of the rest of the group could be put into effect. The changes envisioned by the opening of the cave to the public inevitably would alter the environment and cause the creatures within to move to more remote areas of the cave.

John Schoenherr was our secret weapon. While we had photographs of the cave, maps, and a survey of the twists and turns of the river, we lacked a visual presentation of how it all might look with the changes we were contemplating. As each scheme was agreed upon, it was discussed with John and he produced a picture of how it might look if it actually existed. "Let's put a bridge across the passage here," someone would suggest, and a bridge would appear on John's sketch pad.

John soon discovered that the cave was not the best studio in which to work. The lighting was hopelessly inadequate, the moisture disturbing, and getting into position for the best point of view was sometimes impossible. But by using a Polaroid camera to take a panoramic view of the sections of the cave he

<

The beach at Arecibo. *José Limeres*

wished to sketch, he could get the detail he desired and then could work outside to prepare his finished drawings.

Fortunately, two of the team had no use for their professional skills: nurse Carol Lochner and Dr. José Limeres.

John Spence and Jeannie provided the continuing backup that made the programs and facilities work. John, with his mechanical genius, repaired everything from can openers to thousand-dollar cameras. Jeannie, on the spot, roughed out the publication and consulted with each expedition member so that the resulting reports would be well coordinated in the final presentation.

We had many visits from government and local dignitaries. Our neighbors brought us peppers and squash and would sit and talk with Jeannie. Also the mayors of each of the surrounding towns came to greet us. For a few days we became part of the community, and we seemed to be accepted by all. Our visit was particularly appreciated by the local dogs and cats, who found that Jeannie and Carol were fine providers at the kitchen door.

At the end of the week we decided to take our first tourists for a trip through the cave: I declared the day Ladies' Day. While this would be a return trip for Jeannie, it would be a new experience for Carol, as well as for Jim Storey's wife, Barbara, and Jack Herschend's wife, Sherry, who had just arrived in Puerto Rico.

The women were excellent "tourists," and they seemed to enjoy it so much that Jack Herschend said, "Maybe we don't need all those trails and bridges and the expense of cave development. All we have to do is find girls who don't mind climbing down three hundred feet of ladder over slippery cave walls, wading up to their necks in the river, slipping through mud, and then climbing back out again."

Jack's enthusiasm notwithstanding, the final plan would provide tourists with a three-mile ride in the old sugar train, now with open, shaded, surface cars, starting from the Tres Pueblos Sink and skirting around the haystack hills to a little building near the summit of La Ventosa. There visitors would descend by elevator four hundred feet in thirty seconds to the Natural

Bridge. They would then walk along broad, easy trails forty feet above the river through more than a mile of spectacular passageway, past the Espiral entrance to the Tres Pueblos Sink. There they would enter a tramway that would lift them to the main guest house located on the rim of this spectacular pit.

This arrangement would provide in the space of a few hours an experience not to be duplicated in any other cave in the world. It would provide for millions of people the opportunity to visit one of nature's wonders that only a few of us had been privileged to see. In addition to this exhibition of just a small section of the cave, we would be providing protection for the principal areas for the scientist and explorer who would follow us.

In the meantime, during the ten days of our expedition, José had become intrigued with the tales of the local boys about large fish to be found in the Rio Camuy. He related stories about four-foot eels and three-foot lobsters. Brother Nicholas had searched for them, but found no evidence of any. However, José's interest continued despite our collective disbelief. His determination took him to the local stores in Arecibo, looking for just the right kind of hook, sinker, and line to catch the elusive creatures. He was convinced we were not approaching the problem correctly.

On the last day of the expedition, a few hours before leaving, José slipped off with his carefully selected equipment and a couple of local lads, who took him to their favorite fishing hole at the bottom of the Tres Pueblos sinkhole. He had selected a choice piece of bacon from Carol and dusted it with flour (and I presume made the necessary incantations required for a successful quest). This would be his last chance to make the catch.

Just as we were wondering what had happened to him, José came whooping up the trail swinging a burlap sack over his head. He called to everyone and, with a dramatic flourish, dumped the contents at the feet of a surprised and impressed Brother Nicholas.

A twenty-two inch crayfish emerged, first snapping, then more cautiously weaving its way completely out of the bag. Its body was thicker than a man's wrist.

"The boys tell me this is a small one," he explained happily.

Brother Nicholas bent over and grasped it behind the head, lobster fashion, and put it on the round end of one of the inflated rubber boats that was drying in the sun. Everyone gathered around, and several cameras were being trained on this belligerent, but probably terrified, crayfish.

Cameras snapped and flashbulbs popped, and someone suggested we use something for scale. I picked up a spent flashbulb by the metal end and held it next to one of the slowly weaving claws.

"How's that?" I asked, turning to look at the lens of the camera being focused for a close-up. A loud crunch. My head swung back. I still held the bulb but the claw had whipped out and grasped the glass end, crushing it neatly flat. And I had not felt a thing. I carefully released my grip and respectfully stepped back.

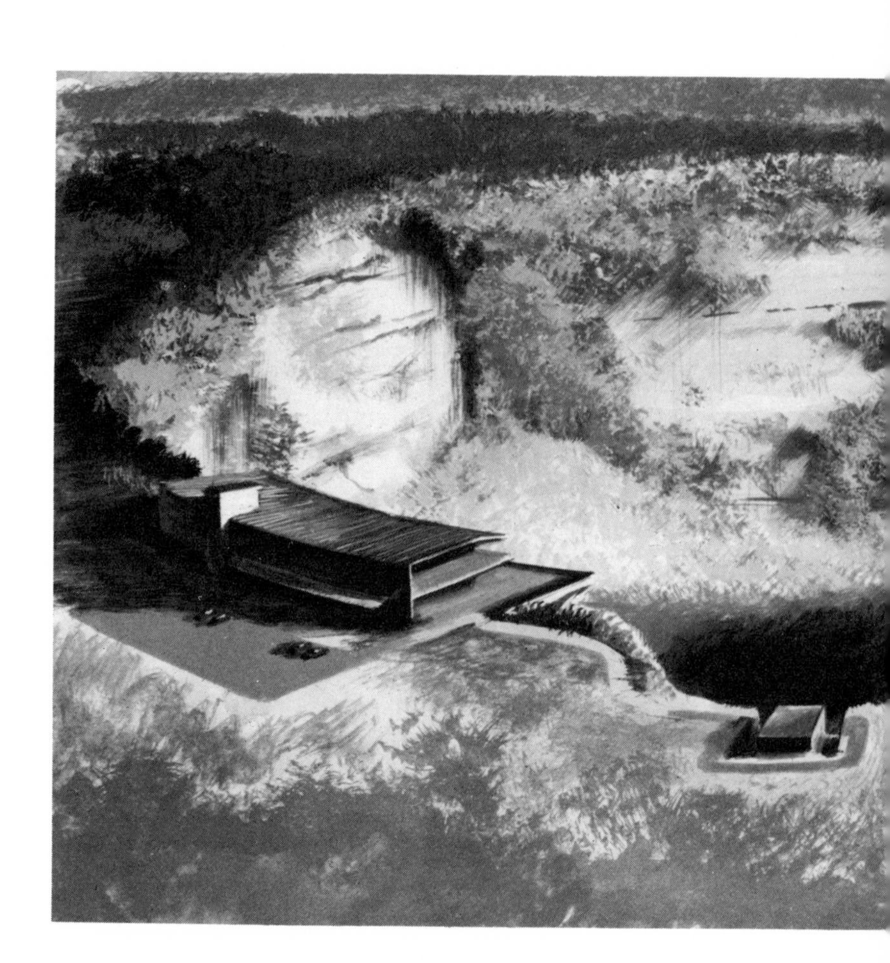

Brother Nicholas later described this bulb masher as a palaemon, *Macrobrachium carcinum,* commonly found in some of the rivers of the island but generally not in caves. It probably had been washed into the underground passages in the flooding. Unfortunately, we had no other specimens to determine whether these creatures had become adapted to the cave. But it was an interesting addition to our collection of life found in the river and cave.

Our expedition ended, we distributed our remaining supplies and food to our very kind neighbors and again headed for home.

Proposed surface facilities at Tres Pueblos sinkhole. *Painting by John Schoenherr*

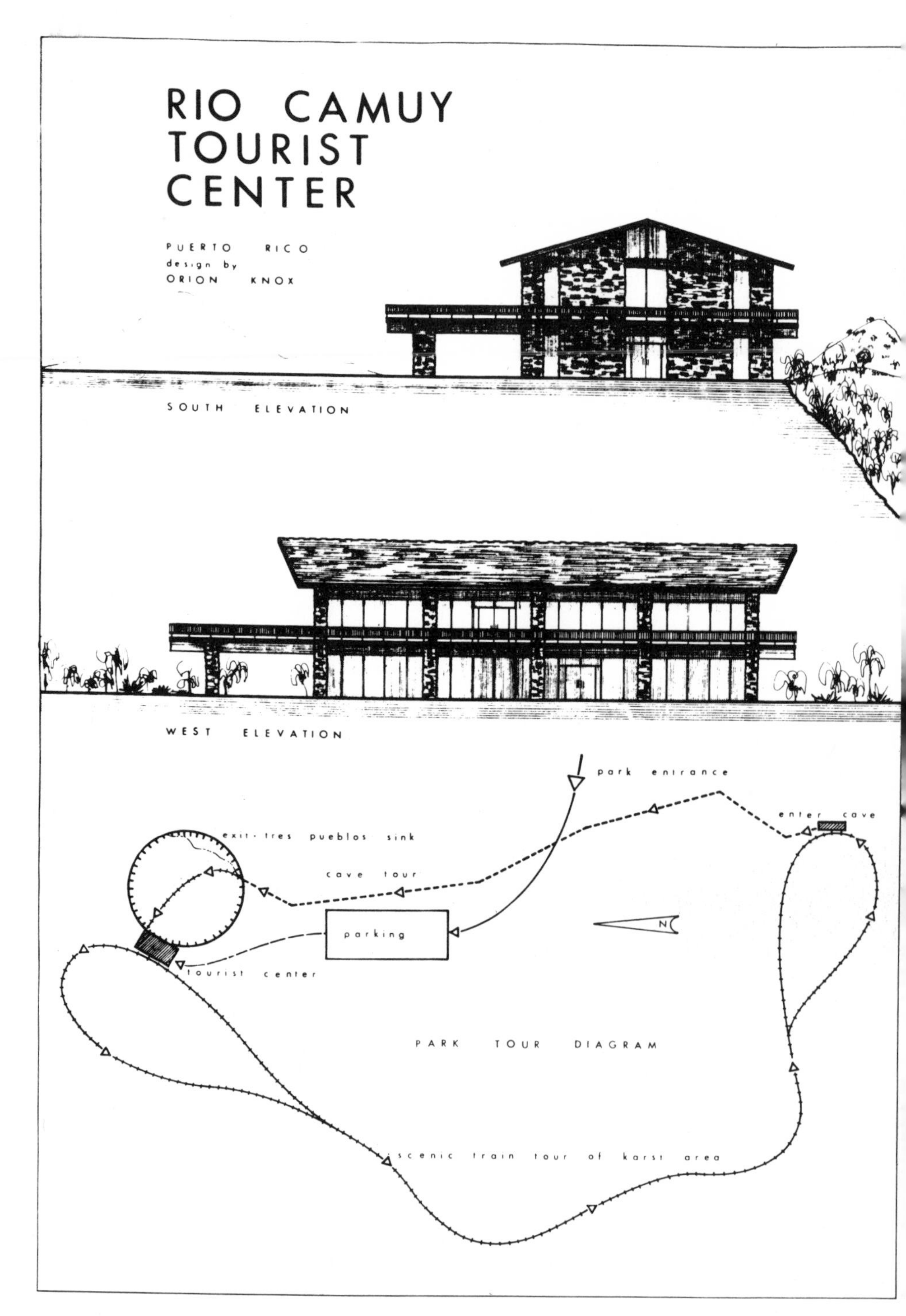

Proposed surface development at Tres Pueblos sinkhole. *Drawing by Orion Knox*

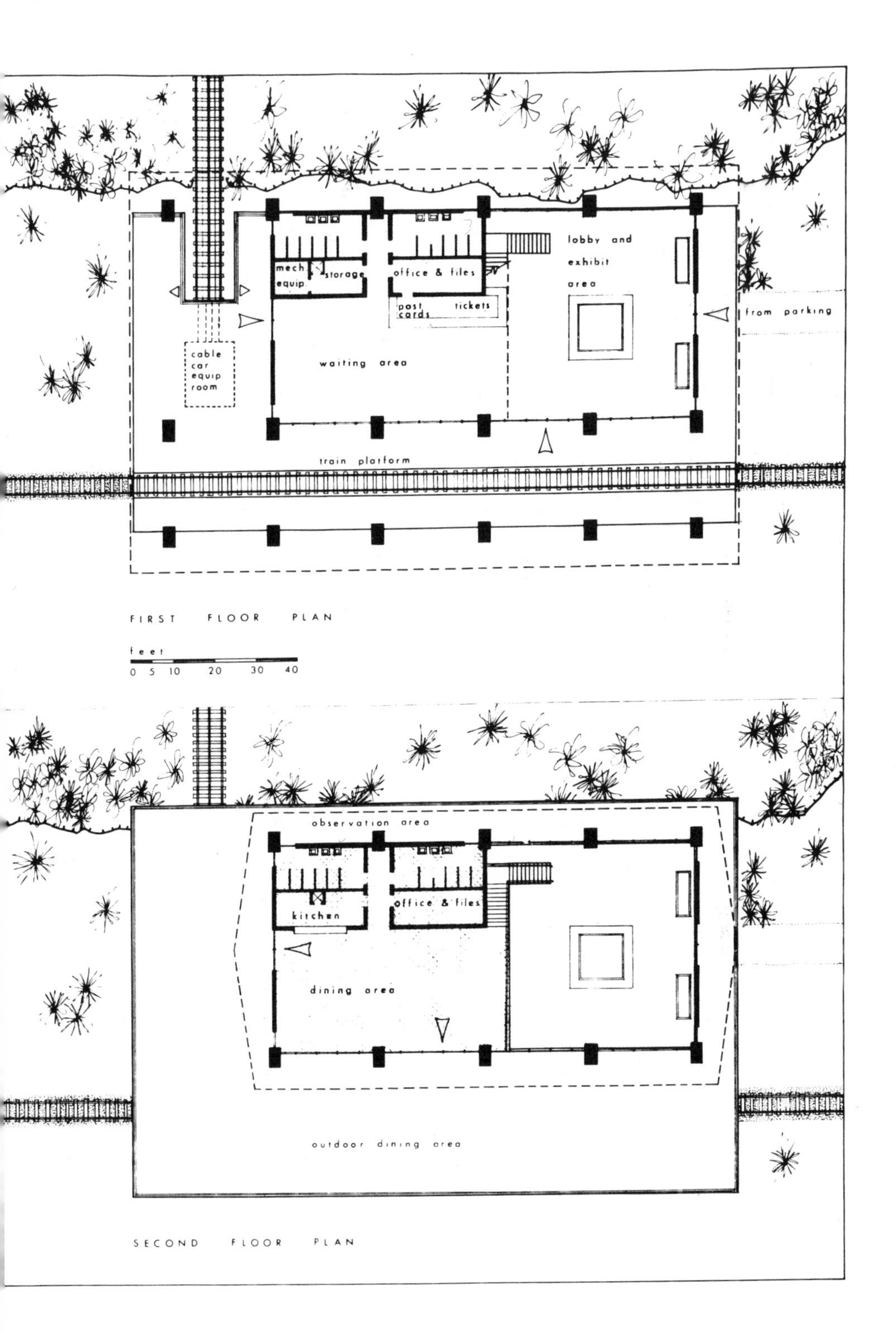
mech equip
storage
office & files
lobby and exhibit area
post cards
tickets
from parking
cable car equip room
waiting area
train platform
FIRST FLOOR PLAN
feet
0 5 10 20 30 40
observation area
office & files
kitchen
dining area
outdoor dining area
SECOND FLOOR PLAN

Proposed bridge beyond the Big Room, for visitors' route.
Painting by John Schoenherr

The Big Room. Tourists will walk between the river and a steep slope of boulders and flowstone. *Painting John Schoenherr*

Espiral entrance with proposed visitors' walkway. River is 40 feet below the trail. *Painting by John Schoenherr*

Canopy formation and rimstone pool along trail. *Painting by John Schoenherr*

chapter VI

It was to be about a year before the Rio Camuy would put us to the ultimate test. In the meantime, we went about our tasks as eagerly as ever.

The burden of the work fell to Jeannie. She had been appointed guest editor of the *Bulletin,* and an entire issue was to be devoted to the Rio Camuy. This meant heavy correspondence, editing, selecting photos, and so on—a full-time job for some months. However, we decided that focusing the *Bulletin* on just one cave was too limited; there was virtually nothing in print on the history and development of show caves in this country. Of course, considerable information on individual caves existed, but very little that tied together the knowledge of how to take a "wild" cave and make it commercial. The purpose of this issue of the *Bulletin* would be to show that viewpoint. It would be directed toward the person who might want to open his cave to the public.

To gather historical information about the famous show caves of the country, we corresponded with cave owners and operators from coast to coast. What we learned was added to what we could get from research and existing cave literature.

The outline of the publication was structured to provide the various steps in developing a cave. As Jeannie and I discussed each step, we prepared a history of work in that area, using the caves of the United States as examples. Then we included the report by the appropriate expert from the Rio Camuy expedition. For example, we showed the development of cave lighting from early torches, candles, and lamps to gas and electric lights, and concluded with Roy Davis's report on lighting recommendations for the Rio Camuy.

When the *Bulletin* was released in April 1967, after more than thirteen months' gestation, an extra one hundred copies were printed and sent to the Puerto Rican government. They seemed pleased, and ordered one thousand more to be distributed among members of the administration and other interested persons. We felt that our work had been quite successful, as both Felix Mejias and Ramon Garcia Santiago assured us that our recommendations regarding the total purchase of the land and zoning of the area would be considered.

After the release of the *Bulletin,* we received a request from the municipality of Aguas Buenas, a small town about ten miles from San Juan, to make a similar study of their cave. The cave was well known in Puerto Rico, and members of the town council and certain landowners felt that it would be economically helpful to open Aguas Buenas to the public.

Our team consisted of Jeannie, Jack Herschend, seven others from the Society, and myself, and our investigation in February 1968 confirmed the cavern's commercial possibilities, but it proved to have a very grave drawback as well. Even though it had a dry upper passage that had been visited for hundreds of years (evidence of Indian occupation inside the entrance indicates it was known before white men came to the island), it also was riddled by a very dangerous fungus, the spores of which are located in the soil. If these spores are inhaled or swallowed, they can cause an acute respiratory disease known as histoplasmosis. The fungus grows within the body as an invasive yeast, forming many small bodies within the cell. In rare cases it may overwhelm the lung and spread throughout the body. Of the seven new members of our Aguas Buenas study group, six who had negative skin tests before the trip were positive afterward—and two of them became seriously ill.

To substantiate our findings, the local Department of Health visited the cave and collected soil samples. These proved positive. The department also took samples in Rio Camuy Cave, but these registered negative. Possibly the flushing action of the river eliminates the conditions suited for the growth of this fungus.

On a more pleasant note, the field trip to Aguas Buenas did provide us with the better acquaintance of several Puerto Rican cavers: Norman Veve and Alan Zague. I was impressed with their enthusiasm—especially that of Norman, who for a long time had had an interest in caves with no one to share it.

Norman was pleased to have the opportunity to work with the group of cavers we had assembled, and it encouraged him to propose the founding of a chapter of the National Speleological Society in Puerto Rico. In the months following the trip, he was already well on the way to getting together a strong, active group of spelunkers.

In the interim, the Rio Camuy report was a matter of public record. The government had proceeded to purchase the land we had recommended—two hundred and fifty acres around the entrances to the Rio Camuy. I still held title to the little farm we had purchased from Sonny Rodriguez, but I agreed to turn the title over to the Commonwealth whenever they desired it. We had achieved the primary goal of our project: the protection of the caves from speculative development and vandalism.

In the summer of 1967 we were notified by the Water Authority that they would be installing a pump in the river near the Empalme entrance. It would provide for the public water supply for the little barrio of Quebrada, nearby. This was a good development as it assured the constant monitoring of the water in the river and would detect any pollution. We felt that all these actions were moving toward the orderly development of the area.

Meantime, Brother Nicholas conducted another student

Indian rock carvings at the entrance to Aguas Buenas Cave. *John Spence*

trip to the cave, adding to the biological knowledge of the region.

Another biologist, Stewart B. Peck, also became interested in the life at the cave. In the fall of 1966, several months after our return, I had received a letter from him saying he was interested in collecting specimens at the Camuy. He asked if he might use the casita as a headquarters for a week in January. I had known Stewart as a spelunker, later as a graduate student at Harvard, and was happy to send him the key. It was a reasonable enough request; we had many friends who wanted to see the area and, since the house was not being used, I felt that lending it to them was a useful and convenient arrangement.

In 1969, I received a reprint of an article Stewart had written in collaboration with John R. Holsinger. It reported in part that, in January 1967, Stewart went into the Empalme Cave and, in a small pool, found a colony of tiny white crustaceans only six millimeters long that proved to be a new genus and species. Magnified, they looked like water fleas—something only a mother could love. He collected 130 specimens and sent them to various institutions for classification and identification. This was routine enough except that, when he realized that this was a new species, he did me great honor of naming the creature *Alloweckelia gurneei.*

That a creature bore my name had an electrifying effect on me. Whereas I had thought of all the bugs and crawling things merely as impedimenta in our search for more cave passage, I now had a sudden warm feeling for these orphaned, isolated, and overlooked crustaceans. Their dismal, solitary existence concerned me, and I became an impassioned advocate for their survival. Stewart's simple, generous act had me studying the sketches and photographs describing the intimate details of my namesakes, which to this day thrive in a seven-inch pool in Empalme Cave.

In March of 1968, Norman Veve, too, asked if he could use the casita as a base of operations. I agreed. The equipment and location of the house would aid his work and help develop an on-site group knowledgeable about the area. I sent him

Alloweckelia gurneei named for the author. *Stewart Peck*

authorization and asked for a release from liability for the Society and me. I also sent him a cautioning letter regarding the hazards of the cave.

On June 17, 1968, I received a newspaper clipping—a feature article from the *San Juan Star*. It was a popular report of a field trip from the Espiral to the Tres Pueblos entrance made by Norman and a group of his friends. While it was a good article, it concerned me and I wrote to Norman:

> This is potentially a dangerous cave. It can be safely explored and safely developed, but it should not become such a casual, easy cave that it ends up like Aguas Buenas—a mass of initials and smoky walls. For this reason I would appreciate it very much if you can avoid newspaper publicity on this particular cave.

Unfortunately, my warning came too late. Before Norman received my letter, the publicity had already set in motion a chain of events that were to involve hundreds of people and affect the cave for some time to come.

At ten o'clock on Sunday night, June 24, 1968, I received a phone call from Puerto Rico from Watson Monroe, a friend and geologist with the United States Geological Survey. He told me that there had been an accident the day before at the Rio Camuy. As he understood it, Norman Veve had taken a group of people—all novices—into the upstream entrance of the Tres Pueblos sinkhole for the purpose of photographing the rimstone pools in the first room. While the group was inside, there was a sudden rise in the water (similar to our previous experiences). Norman told everyone to retreat to the top of Mount Ararat until they could plan what to do. Unfortunately, while Norman was farther on in the cave, two of the group panicked and, with their life jackets inflated, attempted to swim out the entrance with the flow of the surging water. One of the men was able to reach the safety of the shore, but the other, Hector Bueso, aged thirty, was swept along the length of the sinkhole and into the downstream entrance. A few people standing on the shore witnessed this dreadful accident, but were unable to help him; the water was so swift and the action so sudden that he disappeared into the opposite cave entrance as they stood helplessly by.

Norman, with the rest of the party of eight, was not aware of what had happened, and patiently waited about three hours until the water dropped sufficiently to permit a safe exit. They did so by means of a safety line to the people on the outside. As soon as Norman learned of the accident, he went to the entrance where Hector Bueso had disappeared, but it was now flooded with ten feet of water. The torrent was swift and the passage a raging maelstrom; he was not able to enter.

The alarm had been sounded by those outside, but no one in Puerto Rico knew that section of the cave. This placed an impossible burden on Norman, who had no alternative but to wait until the water receded.

He knew that the river reappeared at the bottom of the Empalme sinkhole three thousand feet away, so the next morning he took several men with him and went to that entrance. The river was still high, and he was not able to get even to the waterfall just inside the entrance. The group went back to the Tres Pueblos sinkhole to try lowering a boat on tether into the entrance, but it was too dangerous.

By this time the police were on the scene and the authorities and family knew of the accident. And Norman, as well as Bueso's family, asked that Watson call me.

Watson reassured me that Bueso had a life jacket. That seemed to me to be the important key to the whole story. With a life jacket, a man could safely pass the little choke at the downstream entrance of the Tres Pueblos Sink. But the thought of being swept into a strange, unknown river passage, possibly without lights, and not being able to climb any of the walls or get ashore, was terrifying.

I knew that there was a place eight hundred feet downstream where a man could get out of the water and be safe. I also knew that an exit from the cave was impossible without equipment because of the double waterfall near the Empalme. A lone man in the cave without equipment would be trapped. It was a desperate situation.

I told Watson that there was a chance that Bueso was safe but that since twenty-four hours had already gone by, there was no time to waste. I would come down immediately with boats and equipment.

I called Al Mueller and José Limeres and they agreed

to stand by in case we needed help. Al (who owned a travel agency) arranged passage for me, and I quickly packed my equipment and drove to Kennedy Airport.

It was midnight before I arrived, and I just missed a plane to San Juan. As the next would not leave until 5:00 A.M., I tried to arrange for a military flight from Mitchell Field. However, it was impossible to find one so late on a Sunday night that would go outside the continental limits of the United States.

I called the Puerto Rico phone number Watson had given me and spoke to Hector's brother, Luis. I gave him my time of arrival and he said he would meet me.

When my plane landed the next morning at ten o'clock, Norman Veve, Alan Zague, and several others were at the airport. They had arranged for a ten-man helicopter to take us directly to the cave. I changed into my cave clothes on the field while they rolled out the plane. By noon we touched down in a field next to the Empalme entrance.

So that we could more quickly enter the cave, the Water Authority, which had also provided the helicopter, had alerted the operator of a cable car used for the installation of the pump in the river. We would be lowered by winch to the cave entrance. This installation consisted of a double cable that had been strung across the opening of the Empalme sinkhole. A small open car made of heavy wood planks and protected with a four-foot railing was attached with a pulley arrangement to this cable. We piled the deflated boats, ladders, and rope into this contrivance, and then four of us crouched down on top of this while the superintendent of the waterworks gave the signal to the winch operator.

The cable tightened and we lurched off into space. In a few feet we were carried free over the lip of the sink, and I looked straight down four hundred and fifty feet to the river below. The car moved smoothly ahead and the cable sagged with the weight until we reached the center of the 150-foot-wide opening. Then the pulley hit a stop on the cable and the car shuttered and started to descend. In seconds we were out of sight of the winch and the operator. We went down swiftly into the mouth of this huge, juglike hole, and just when it seemed as if we were going to crash at the bottom, the descent slowed and we eased to a stop on a cleared level platform next to the river.

We unloaded all the equipment and walked down a smooth trail to a boardwalk that had been put into the cave to permit workmen to get to the water pump. This platform provided an excellent place to inflate the boats, so I upended the two sacks I had brought and dumped them out.

There were several men waiting for us, and they immediately began to pump up the boats while I took out the extra carbide lights I had brought. Norman, Alan Zague, and I prepared to light them. I asked for another man to accompany us, and Norman introduced me to muscular and sturdy Tito Zambrana, who said he was a friend of Hector Bueso.

I looked at my watch; it was now 1:00 P.M. The accident had occurred almost exactly forty-four hours before.

The river was high and I could see the evidence that it had been over the boardwalk recently. From past experience I guessed that it was only about three feet deep at this point; the water was so coffee-colored it was impossible to see the bottom.

I threw one of the boats into the water and asked Tito to come with me. Norman and Alan followed in the other boat. We swiftly paddled upstream to the pool where the waterfall was noisily splashing. I beached the boat, motioned to Tito to follow, and climbed over the boulders that hid the passage to the top of the waterfall. I was now looking at the climb that Orion Knox and Roy Davis had made to rig the passage for the first traverse of this part of the cave (the original rigging had been removed when we left). I had never entered this way but had only descended it on the way back that one time with Roy, Orion, and José two years before. What a long time ago that seemed! The route upward looked as smooth and as steep as a child's slide and impossible to climb. It was a narrow cleft in the rocks two to three feet wide, floored with flowstone and sloping up at a forty-five-degree angle. There was not a handhold visible its entire length. I felt a clutch in the pit of my stomach. I thought, "I haven't done any climbing in a while. What if I can't make this?"

Taking the sack of climbing hardware I had brought, I took out a geologist's pick. A blow at the flowstone caused it to ring like a bell. By now, Norman and Alan came alongside and the four of us silently looked at the obstacle ahead.

I took our sixty feet of $\frac{7}{16}$-inch rope, tied it around my waist, and started to climb. The only way possible was to chimney up the crack—my back pressing against one side and my feet the other. The first twenty feet were easy, the next twenty a little harder. I was now firmly wedged into the crevice, but the space had narrowed to about two feet, and I could not move without becoming almost vertical. The backside of the crevice was no help as it was smooth and wet. I could not cling to that. The wall extended about ten feet more to the top, but it looked as smooth as glass. I wondered if I could hold on.

I glanced down at the three lights below. "Can you throw me a hammer, Norman?"

I pushed myself outward, away from the slope, and in a few seconds the hammer came sliding up beneath me. I stopped it and began to peck away at the calcite. I found a spot that sounded dead and, turning the pointed side down, chipped away some of the stone until I could wedge it into the crevice. The hammer was secure, so I pulled myself up to where I could put my foot on its head and stand.

But I was still not high enough to reach the top. I remembered that there were several stubby stalagmites just over the crest, so I took the rope from my waist, doubled it in a loop and made several casts over the edge. Finally I snagged something. I cautiously put my weight on the double rope. It held. Clinging close to the slope so that I wouldn't dislodge the loop, I pulled myself over the edge.

It took only a minute to tie a ladder to the rope so the others could climb up and join me.

As soon as Alan made it he started to haul up a boat and extra rope and ladder to rig the other side. When we all had reached the top, we went over to the edge of the upstream waterfall and called, showed our lights, and listened. There was no sound but the rushing water.

The disappointment was obvious to all of us. I looked at Norman and realized the anguish he must be suffering. I de-

>

Russell Gurnee canyon-hopping. *José Limeres*

scribed the next room to all three and then suggested that Norman and I take the boat ahead and leave Alan and Tito on the top to help us up when we returned.

I secured the ladder, tied a safety rope on my waist, and started down. When I reached the bottom, Alan and Tito lowered the boat (which I was careful to keep out of the waterfall this time), and got in and waited for Norman. He soon joined me and we pushed off to the sandy beach that I remembered was on this side of the falls. The beach was now at least three feet deep in water; the level was still quite high.

We called again as we started into the Bat Room. The sound echoed, but there was no answer. We carried the boat over the portage, carefully scanning the river for signs of Hector as we went. Leaving the boat so we could hurry ahead, we were soon at the water passage.

At each point we saw and heard nothing but the rushing of the water and the echoing of our voices.

"There is only one place he can be," I said. "There is another flowstone choke about six hundred feet upstream; and it would be the only way to get out of the water between here and the Tres Pueblos entrance."

Then I looked at my watch. It was six o'clock. Norman had not slept for at least forty-eight hours and he looked exhausted. Also, that chimney had taken more out of me than I liked to admit. I knew we were not equipped to make the passage.

"We'll have to go back," I said. "If it doesn't rain tonight, we'll come through the Tres Pueblos entrance and search out the rest of the cave at daybreak tomorrow."

On the way out we searched the room to be sure there was nothing we had missed. Then we climbed the waterfall and exited the cave.

At the entrance there were still a large group of people awaiting word. We had nothing to offer but the hope that we might have better success the next day. Luis had made arrangements to take us to Lares, where we ate and tried to get some sleep.

It was an anxious night for all of us, and at daylight we were heading back to the cave. Norman had not been able to sleep, and although he felt he could continue with us, I persuaded him that he would be of more value on the outside in case we needed any assistance from a support party.

There was a superabundance of helpful people present who were willing to aid in any capacity. I asked Norman if there was a physician present, and he introduced me to Dr. José Martinez, an athletic-looking, dark-haired man with a moustache. The doctor was a good friend of Hector and, while he had never been in a cave, he was a scuba diver and anxious to do whatever he could to help.

We now had Alan, who was experienced, Tito, who had proved to be excellent the day before, Dr. Martinez, and myself.

As we were about to launch the boats I noticed that the water had dropped considerably from the night before. Therefore, we should have no trouble with headroom, although the current still looked swift and angry as we peered down the throat of the tunnel ahead.

Just then Alan took me aside and in a low voice whispered, "What are our chances of coming out of this alive?"

I was stunned. It hadn't occurred to me what great courage these men were showing to venture into this awful swallow hole. It must have seemed to them sheer recklessness. Yet they were willing to do this for the love of a friend. It made a profound impression on me.

I didn't answer Alan directly but called for the other two men to join us. I said, "Let me assure you that what we are about to do is perfectly safe. If I had any concern that we were on a suicide mission, we would not be here. I have a wife and two daughters and have every intention of seeing them again this week."

It was their turn to look a little stunned, but it was something that had to be said. After all, they didn't know me, and their safety was in my hands. I was equipped with previous knowledge of the route ahead; they had to rely solely on my judgment.

The meeting ended and I called to Norman to have someone meet us at the top of the waterfall at 2:00 P.M. to help haul up the boats and belay the men out.

Dr. Martinez was in the front boat, so I stepped in and

pushed off boldly into the full stream. We were off with the current on a Nantucket sleigh ride right down the center of the water passage. Alan and Tito followed. We had to duck our heads as we went through the lowest arch to clear the stalactites that hung like multiple tonsils in a black throat. The light from the entrance was suddenly gone and we were in pitch blackness. We stopped paddling and waited for Alan and Tito to come alongside. The passageway was wider here and the water was still and deep. We checked our carbide lights and began anxiously searching along the walls and sides of the passage.

We were only about two hundred feet from the entrance, but the ceiling here was more than a hundred feet above us. We were drifting through a twenty-foot-wide crevice with flanking walls rising at least eighty feet without a break as far as we could see. There was some vertical fluting, but nothing at the waterline—no projections that would permit a swimming man to hang on or climb.

I pushed my paddle straight down into the water, up to my elbow, without touching bottom. We were drifting quite rapidly and since it wasn't necessary to paddle we used our flashlights freely to probe everywhere.

We were approaching the blockage in the passage I had referred to when we turned back the day before. It was the first location at which a person would be able to get ashore. We shined our lights ahead, and saw what appeared to be a solid, blank wall. We silently paddled toward it. About fifty feet away we entered a surface covering of foam—possibly the residue from detergents used upstream by local washerwomen. These suds were several inches thick and were laced with bamboo poles, branches, and twigs that had been trapped there.

In the middle of this mass of flotsam I saw a gray floating object. We paddled into the mess, and I reached out and picked up an inflated life jacket. The snaps were unhooked and the ribbons were untied. It could not have been worn at the time he was swept in.

Both boats were now in the suds, and we began to rake the surface with one of the bamboo poles. There appeared to be nothing else floating on the surface. Dr. Martinez climbed out of the boat onto a flowstone slope and he continued up the wall to a crevice about eight feet above the water. This was the only possible spot for a man to get out of the water between here and Tres Pueblos, where Hector had gone in. There was nothing.

We all knew then that there was no hope of finding him alive. The discovery of the life jacket, which would have kept him afloat, was the staggering evidence that he could not have survived.

Until now, the possibility that he might have been trapped on this miserable perch above the river had kept us hurrying to get here. Now the realization that he could never have reached here alive came as a leaden blow; it dashed hopes and dulled urgency. The reaction of Hector's friends was penetrating—prolonged, deep silence. Alan and Tito just sat in their boat with paddles shipped, and foam slowly formed around the stern as the current gently pushed everything toward the barrier in the passage; Dr. Martinez was out of the boat squatting on his heels, seeing nothing, just a few feet above us.

I broke the silence: "Without his life jacket, he didn't have a chance." This obvious conclusion brought no response, so I tried again: "The burden of this search is going to be on you men. I will help, but in the end you must be satisfied that we have done everything possible to eliminate any chance that we may have missed him. Tomorrow, when I return to the States, there should be no doubt in your minds that we looked everywhere."

For the next half hour we probed the pool with the bamboo poles—a grim and depressing procedure. We checked every portion of the pool, but we were not able to reach the bottom even with a twenty-foot-long splintered section that Alan found. The flowstone barrier that choked the passage extended down four to six feet beneath the surface. There was nothing.

We portaged over the barrier, taking along several eight-foot poles, and continued our search as we drifted slowly downstream. The continuation of the passage was similar to the first eight hundred feet. There was no place along the walls to get ashore. Neither were there any obstructions that might have trapped a man. Apparently the blockage we had just passed trapped all floating material, until it became waterlogged and settled to the bottom, where it was flushed out in the periodic flooding.

The strange environment and grim search were etching an unforgettable picture in the minds of each of us. To these men who knew Hector it was traumatic; to me it was sobering and extremely depressing. Caves to me had always been fascinating and mysterious places. Through the years I had explored thousands of caves, and I had come to feel a certain comfort and security in the stillness and sanctity of a cave. This particular passage had pleasant memories for me. We had once made a fun trip here with good companions. Now it had become a fearful place—the scene of a dreadful accident. I had difficulty rationalizing to myself that this was the same cave and that the search we were making was actually happening.

My reverie was broken by the murmur of rapids ahead. In a few minutes we turned a bend and the full sound of rushing water burst upon us. We back-paddled to stop our slow drift and flashed our lights ahead. We were approaching the end of the Bat Room, and our lights were swallowed up in the blackness ahead. The sound that had bestirred me was coming from the water pouring over a small waterfall.

We paddled over to the shore where we could easily get out of the boats and begin our portage through the room. This was the spot where Norman and I, coming in the opposite direction, had turned back the previous night. We had now made the final connection through the cave and had found only the life jacket.

"Norman and I searched this room last night," I said, "but we will have to do it again more thoroughly."

The next hour and a half was even more painful than before, the worst I have ever experienced in a cave. In this huge room, enveloped by the sound of rushing water, fluttering, disturbed bats, and flickering headlamps, we probed every possible rock and overhang along both sides of the river. We checked the pools with bamboo poles; looked under ledges and logs that had snagged on obstructions along the way; and found nothing.

Finally, we were out of the room and in sight of the Empalme waterfall. Just as we were preparing to launch the boat in that direction, we saw a light and heard a call from the top of the waterfall. It was Norman and his party come to help us with the equipment and boats.

The four of us were very depressed knowing we could do no more. We had proved through our best efforts that Hector was not in the cave. We pulled all our equipment over the falls and exited through the Empalme entrance.

I quietly explained to Hector's wife the failure of our search, gave the life jacket to Luis, and extended my sympathies. There was nothing else to be said.

The group was disbanded. That evening, in San Juan, among all the people who had been present on the day of the accident was the photographer who had been taking motion pictures of the group and the rimstone pool. He had already developed his film and spliced it so that it was possible for us to see Hector Bueso preparing to enter the cave. Hector had on a hard hat, carried a flashlight, and wore the gray life jacket we had found in the cave. A rope used as a safety line stretched across the entrance pool, and each person wore a life jacket and a hard hat. There was no question in my mind that the organization and planning for the trip were normal.

Even now, Norman Veve remained greatly shocked and depressed by the whole affair. He assumed responsibility for the tragedy to a degree I thought unfair to himself. As the leader of the group he had conducted them well, specifically telling them to wait at the top of Mount Ararat as the river flooded. His order was not carried out, and the chain of events that followed resulted in the tragedy.

There was only one point that disturbed me regarding the trip. That was the initial purpose of the Sunday afternoon visit to the cave. As I reconstructed it, the events occurred something like this:

The Land Administration (the department that purchased the property around the cave) was preparing a report of its work on the island. Felix Mejias, director, had commissioned a photographer to illustrate this report. He was to photograph the various purchases and projects of the department and prepare a visual record, with blanket permission to visit and film what he liked. One of the areas he thought would be interesting to show was the Rio Camuy project. He contacted Norman, told him that he had permission to visit the cave, and asked if Norman would lead him.

Assuming that it would involve only the photographer and a few other people, he agreed.

But on the day of the trip, seventeen arrived. It is possible that the publicity in the newspaper contributed to the large turn-out. However, Norman did not have enough equipment for them all, and insisted that only adults with proper gear could enter. This amounted to twelve people.

He took all the precautions necessary for the group to safely visit the cave, but misjudged their ability. There was no way for Norman to predict the flash flooding and the reaction to this emergency.

The next day I called Felix Mejias on the telephone to tell him what had happened. He was shocked. I asked him if he knew of the trip to the cave, and he said that he had not been aware of it. The permission he had given the photographer had included the Rio Camuy project, but he did not know of that particular trip.

I left the island convinced that the tragedy had resulted from one of those curious combinations of circumstances that appear innocuous at first, but suddenly build up to produce a fatal conclusion. Norman was no more responsible than are we all when we venture into the unknown and take others with us.

chapter VII

I never expected that the luxury liner *Queen Elizabeth* would have anything to do with this story, but she did play a small though important part.

I hadn't heard from Norman Veve since that time in June 1968, until a letter arrived the following March. A member of the Puerto Rican House of Representatives, Señor Anibel Vázquez Negron, had gotten in touch with him regarding the work done at the Rio Camuy. He was preparing to present a bill to fund the development of the cave. The bill proposed that the government commit money for this in terms of its becoming a park for the people of Puerto Rico and an attraction for tourists to the island. Covered in a news clipping he had enclosed was much discussion, and several unrelated bills were proposed in an attempt to improve the health of the tourist industry. One was for the purchase of the *Queen Elizabeth,* then up for sale, to be used as a floating boatel. The world's largest passenger ship until the 1950s, she was to be made into a convention center.

Later I learned that this bill won out, and four million dollars was bid for the craft—which was bought for $8.6 million by someone else. In the meantime, the bill to develop the caves had failed and the ship was taken to Hong Kong. Three years later it burned and sank.

Activity at the cave, however, continued as Norman explored some of the other possibilities around the area. Also, he had found that others were interested in the project. One was Dr. Graham Nelson, astronomer at the radiotelescope in Arecibo, active speleologist from Australia, and past president of the Blue Mountain Speleological Society in Sydney.

Nelson, sometimes with Norman, sometimes with a friend from the observatory, spent many days hiking the trails near the cave. In a few months he had accumulated reports and accounts of many of the caverns of the region. He would be helpful in another way, too.

One of our objectives had been to locate the resurgence of the river. This seemed as if it would be a simple project, but each time we had sent a party to attempt to locate it, what they found always left a nagging doubt about whether or not it was actually the main river. The watercourse seen from the air seemed to follow the canyon of the Camuy; but on closer examination the little stream that emerged from the canyon did not quite justify its being the continuation of the Camuy. Finally Norman, with Graham Nelson and several others, decided to go upstream in the canyon and find where the river might be reappearing. They were rewarded with the discovery of a large flow of water coming from a ten-foot-high opening in the side of the canyon. It was possible to wade and swim into this passage to a series of chambers and, finally, to a breakdown where the water appeared to flow through. But it was impossible to continue.

This seemed to provide an explanation regarding the resurgence, namely, that there might be several exits for the water. Further exploration upstream could possibly permit penetration to the Empalme Cave. This new opening put the possible length of the entire underground route of the Camuy at a little over four air miles. This would undoubtedly mean that the Camuy flowed a twisted course of at least seven miles as it traveled beneath the limestone. The speculation for the number of miles of cave passage is staggering when the hundreds of square miles of limestone in this portion of the island are considered.

Nelson then continued his researches without Norman. On December 20, 1969, with two friends, Leroy Cogger and Gus Zeissig, he tried a location one-half mile southwest of Ventosa suggested by Watson Monroe as a possible access to the underground river. Watson and I had seen this hole from the air. However, although we circled low over it in our small plane, we could not add anything but that it was very deep.

Nelson explored the hole and discovered that it penetrated to the water level and, also, that the level resembled the river at the bottom of the Tres Pueblos sinkhole—though the hole was smaller and not so exposed, but just as exciting to explore.

The men were without swimming gear, but were able to see that this was a major discovery. The local farmer who owned the property acknowledged that the river in the cave was called Rio de los Angeles. However, he did not connect it with the Rio Camuy even though he was familiar with the exploration that had been done only a few miles away.

When they returned, Nelson and Gus, with Norman, called this new location Angeles Cave, and within the next few weeks, they pushed its exploration nearly five thousand feet upstream, mapping as they went.

Norman and Nelson developed a system of travel in these water caves that both amazed and distressed me. They had discovered that the use of life jackets alone could provide the safety and speed to permit them to cover great areas. This method worked well for them, and their results were certainly impressive. Fully dressed with boots, helmet, and lamp, they managed to be supported by a kapoc life jacket and swim several hundred feet along the underground channel of the river. This can be strenuous, as it is generally necessary to hold one hand out of the water to keep dry those items that will not fit under a helmet. I have tried it and cannot say it is my favorite pastime. It should not be a recommended method for novices.

Here is Nelson's description of one of his penetrations of the Angeles system. It may never become popular:

> An incredible mass of logs, coconuts, and general rubbish floated on the surface of the water, but there was about 9″ of

> clearance to the roof, so I was able to swim through into the room beyond. This room was about eighty feet high and twenty feet in diameter, but there appeared to be no obvious way out. There would have been no way of crossing the room anyway because it was completely choked with logs up to six feet deep. The logs were slimy, usually with one end in the water and the other resting on the wall. The whole mess was incredibly unstable and dangerous so I quickly retreated back through the sump to join the others.

In January 1970 I received an enthusiastic letter from Norman about the discovery, and I plotted it on the topographic map. The underground course of the river was taking shape and the explorations now began to show the culmination of eleven years of work. Starting at the Empalme entrance, we had a solid line extending about two miles to the end of the West Tributary, just upstream of La Ventosa, a gap, and then the Angeles segment discovered by Norman and Nelson that extended almost another mile.

Where would this lead? It was now time to look again at the first cave we had visited in 1958, La Cueva del Humo, southwest of Blue Hole, for the passage in Angeles pointed directly toward the main passage in Humo.

Nelson and Norman had anticipated me, however, for their next report, in May of 1970, covered a visit to Humo. From there, they had extended their explorations to within five hundred feet of the known portions of Angeles. In the process, they had explored several blind leads, tried to follow the river, which pinched out, and climbed the slippery, muddy walls to push on beyond a sump that required more equipment and manpower than they possessed.

This spurt of interest was to suffer a delay, however: Graham completed his tour of duty at the radiotelescope in Arecibo and returned to Australia and Norman suffered from an attack of gout that was certainly not improved by his exertion and extended dunkings in the river. The continued exploration of the cave would have to await not only Norman's recovery, but also another stable of cavers as interested as he.

It wasn't long. At Easter time, 1970, two British cavers,

David and Shirley St. Pierre, in Puerto Rico on holiday, got in touch with Norman and Watson Monroe. The fame of the cave had spread and anyone within reasonable traveling distance made it (and the hospitality of the local people) a point of destination.

This experienced couple was taken for a tour (Norman's health had improved somewhat) of the main trunk of the Camuy and treated to a further exploration in Angeles Cave. This was evidently enough to infect them with the fever of the place, for they pledged to return in "dry season" (whatever that might mean at the Rio Camuy).

Forces were building up, however, from several quarters that would culminate in further attention to the Camuy. In June 1971, I attended the National Speleological Society convention in Blacksburg, Virginia, and at the conclusion of the banquet I was approached by a young girl who said she wanted to lead a trip to the Rio Camuy. She introduced herself as Emily Davis, a student at Franklin Pierce College. She explained that she had established a caving group at the college and wanted to do some work in Puerto Rico. We spoke briefly about it, and I gave her the names of Norman Veve and Watson Monroe and told her that they were doing active work there and should be able to help her.

In the meantime I had shifted my attention in Puerto Rico to another river that flowed through the same karst area, the Rio Tanama. It is larger than the Camuy and a few miles east of where we had been working. I had considered this river for exploration many years before, but the volume of work at the Camuy had distracted me. However, since my last visit, there was a good and compelling reason to look at the Tanama: The deposit of copper ore that had been discovered in the early sixties southeast of the Camuy area—estimated at one and a half billion dollars—was being let by the Commonwealth to commercial interests to mine and develop. Obviously the environmental impact, including the disposal of the residue—slurry from the mine—would be a serious consideration. One suggestion was to put the waste into the sinkhole country just east of the Camuy. But the United States Geological Survey had made a ground water study of the region and proved an underground connection between the drainage of the sinkholes and the Tanama River. (The river ultimately became the principal water supply for the city of Arecibo on the north coast.)

Apparently the results of this study did not satisfy the engineers who were planning the disposal of the wastes, and another survey was made in 1970. This time helicopters were used for surface reconnaissance. However, from the aerial photographs, the river disappeared underground five times in its thirteen-mile course to the ocean, for most of which it flowed at the bottom of a deep canyon so narrow in places that the trees made a canopy, preventing surveillance from the air. It would be necessary to float down the river, go through the caves, and sample the springs along the way in order to make a more thorough study of the ground water flow.

This seemed too good an opportunity to pass up, so I planned a trip down the river with several of the men who had been on the Camuy expeditions: Roy Davis, because of his ability with rope work, Jack Herschend, as an old Missouri white-water river enthusiast, and Ad Austin, a fellow caver, club member, and pilot. I contacted the United States Geological Survey about the proposed trip and got an enthusiastic response from Don Jordan, chief of the Caribbean area. He volunteered himself and suggested another man from the Survey, Vito Latkovitch.

We selected five days early in December because it was the end of the rainy season. We hoped this period would give us enough water, but not too much. However, it was certainly not a canoe stream—in fact we wondered whether we would be able to do it in rubber boats.

The level of the river was easy to identify from the several locations accessible on foot, but the gradient was 860 feet in 10 miles of travel—an average of 86 feet to the mile (a "normal" white-water river drops 10 to 15 feet to a mile).

The trip was all we could have hoped for. The rapids were clean and swift, the scenery was magnificent, and the water plunged through nine uncharted caves enroute. We camped in small caves along the canyon and in three days emerged at the lower end of the Tanama—the first traverse of this wild, beautiful region of Puerto Rico.

This left us with one more day in Puerto Rico. We still had our equipment and some energy, so I suggested we see Angeles Cave.

Norman Veve joined us. He had not been caving for some months, and was still suffering from gout in one leg, but his handicap wouldn't stop him.

The entrance to Angeles Cave was as spectacular as any of the other deep sinks of the Camuy, and I realized why so many people had developed an interest in it. The river was smaller, but the expanse of the rooms was breathtaking. While Roy, Jack, Vito, Ad, and Norman went ahead, I mapped as I followed—the first two thousand feet resembling a huge subway tunnel.

We all had life jackets, and I was introduced to the dubious pleasure of Norman's swim technique as we swam 127 breast strokes through the deep water of the long passages. We passed the first pool and I was able to keep my sketch pad dry, but the second pool discouraged me. I stopped mapping at the 2500-foot mark and relaxed to enjoy the scenery of the last half of the cave.

We entered a huge room nearly a mile from the entrance, known and mapped by Norman and Nelson. They called it the Final Room. I was beginning to feel the exertions of the previous three days on the river, so I waited at the top of a huge mound while Jack and Roy went ahead to an impassable sump. This was the end of the trip for us, but it was possible that with additional equipment we could have gone farther.

The trip out was more enjoyable. We photographed some of the fine rimstone pools and were treated to the splendid view through the green foliage at the bottom of the Angeles entrance. As we exited, Norman told me of the plans coming up in connection with the cave.

Brother Nicholas was planning to send a group down to the area in January; Emily Davis had arranged for a group from Franklin Pierce College, David and Shirley St. Pierre were also planning to visit within the next month. It appeared there would be some excellent accomplishments in the near future.

In January 1972, the three groups were assembled at the Camuy cave area for the beginning of an exciting month. Emily Davis had succeeded, through much correspondence, in contacting everyone on the island interested in the Camuy, Brother Nicholas had assembled a group of students and two experienced cavers from Tennessee, and the St. Pierres had arranged to come over from their vacation in the Virgin Islands to help out.

Emily, a junior in college, had arrived with faculty advisor Ed Zawlocki and three students: Tom Beardsley, Henry Boenning, and Keith Irwin. Equipped with tents, food, and cooking gear, they had rented a car and had set up camp in the open field near the Empalme entrance. The St. Pierres and their children had joined them. Also, Francis McKinney and Forest Miller, the experienced cavers from Oak Ridge, Tennesse, spent a few days, providing mapping and climbing assistance; the students worked in the same area.

Norman, who was suffering from his trip into the caves with my party several weeks before, had to be content with providing backup and any information the group might desire.

The group decided that what needed the most attention was the possibility of joining Cueva del Humo with Angeles (which Norman and Nelson had come short of by five hundred feet). This was a big enough project to occupy them entirely, but the task of mapping the cave would take up the first few days.

In two parties they entered from each end—Humo and Angeles—surveying the passage as they went. Each reached the difficult sumps that had stopped Norman and Nelson just two years before. Their separate surveys showed, however, that they were less than four hundred feet apart, so in company with Miller and McKinney, the group from Pierce College concentrated on trying to rig this treacherous area. The section that presented the obstacle was a chamber ankle deep in guano, with a level ceiling—but the floor was pitted with holes thirty feet deep. These pits belled out so that it was necessary to rig them with wire ladders in order to navigate them safely.

The Pierce party, entering the Humo entrance, reached the most remote part of the cave. On the lip of the mud slope that led up to the last impenetrable pit they left a plastic Coolite—

a chemical luminescent light similar to that of a firefly—that would glow in the dark for about three hours. It was hoped that the party entering from the Angeles entrance would be able to see it from the opposite side of the pit.

The next day, the Pierce party, reinforced with the St. Pierres, switched to the Angeles entrance and rigged two more pits. This entailed cutting steps in the mud in places, using assorted pieces of scrap metal for pitons, and some tricky climbs by Ed Zawlocki. The final spot reached looked familiar to Ed, but there was no sign of the Coolite that had been left the day before. They duplicated the experiment, this time setting up the beacon on the guano-covered floor in Angeles, and returned to the entrance.

According to their survey, they should have connected. But two days later Emily Davis, Ed Zawlocki, Tom Beardsley, Keith Irwin, and Henry Boenning entered the Humo and spotted the surprisingly still-burning Coolite left by Zawlocki. Emily's party did not continue on through to make the traverse, however, as they did not have the necessary equipment at the moment.

This brought to a close the exploration on this portion of the cave. All that remained was to complete the maps and put the information together. Although there were a few more sorties to other leads in the area—another look at the resurgence north of Empalme—the big problem had been solved. Nearly two miles of continuous passage had been added to the known portion of the Camuy cave system. It now exceeded more than six miles of main river passage. These were all large tunnels; none of the crawlways or small passages had been added.

The cave system continues to grow each time a party concentrates on the exploration of the Camuy. It will be many years before we have a complete picture of the passages that must twist and turn beneath this huge limestone area of Puerto Rico.

In October 1972, Jeannie and I again visited the island, and I conferred with the Department of Public Works, the agency assigned to the protection of the cave and the area now owned by the government. I also met Roberto Vásquez (assistant secretary of the Department of Natural Resources) and Pedro Tirado (director of the Office of Scientific Inventory) and discussed the work done on the cave, including the recent discoveries in Angeles. We were joined by Sergio Cautino, working directly with the protection of the caves and natural phenomena of the island.

If, as planned, the Administration elevates the Department of Natural Resources to make it a bureau of the government, this will provide a greater opportunity for its division of Public Works to pursue the protection of the natural heritage of the island. Perhaps it will also bring the Rio Camuy caves closer to development and exhibition for the enjoyment and benefit of all people.

GLOSSARY

BELAY—*v.* To secure a climber by tying a rope around him from above. *n.* The rope supported above by a climber and/or some sturdy object.

BRAKE BAR—Climbing hardware. A small metal ladder-shaped contrivance used to provide sufficient friction on a rope to permit controlled descent.

BREAKDOWN—Broken rock, usually fractured and angular in shape, which has fallen from the ceiling of a cave.

BROOMSTICKS—Tall, thin stalagmites.

CALCITE (*or* CALCIUM CARBONATE)—The principal content of stalactites and stalagmites. In its pure form it is crystalline and transparent and known for its ability to produce double refraction of light.

CARBIDE (*or* CALCIUM CARBIDE)—When mixed with water this chemical compound decomposes and produces acetylene gas. When ignited, the combination in a proper lamp will provide a safe, dependable source of light.

CAVE FORMATIONS—Any secondary deposits in a cave, usually drip-formed calcite or other mineral growths that are found on the ceiling, walls, or floor of a cave. Examples: Stalactites, stalagmites, mud or clay fill, helictites, and flowstone.

CAVE PEARLS—The "pearls" are formed as calcite accumulates around pebbles in pools. These small balls do not adhere to the bottom of the pool because of the movement of the water, and the pearls grow as they are gently rocked and turned therein.

CHIMNEY—A method of climbing a narrow, vertical crevice. The distance between the crevice must permit the climber to have his back against one side and his feet against the other. He climbs by alternating his weight against his shoulders, arms, and feet.

CHOKE—A barrier that effectively obstructs further passage.

COMMERCIAL CAVE—A cave open to the public for an admittance fee. Often the cave is modified with lights and trails for the convenience of visitors. Also called a "show cave" or "tourist cave."

CUL-DE-SAC—A dead end. A French term literally translated as the "bottom of a bag."

EXPANSION BOLTS—Climbing hardware. Metal fasteners that may be attached to a solid stone wall by drilling a hole with a star drill and inserting a metal plug.

FLOWSTONE—General term for calcite growth on the floor, walls, and sometimes ceiling of a cave and known as a secondary growth (*See* CAVE FORMATIONS). It has been dissolved from limestone in rock found above the deposit.

HAYSTACK—A popular term for conical-shaped hills in tropical limestone regions. The combination of solution and erosion has shaped these hills out of a plain or plateau (also called mogotes, kegelkarst, and pepino hills).

HELICTITES—Erratic and twisted cave formations (q.v.) that seem to defy gravity. They can be found in the most improbable shapes. The actual method of formation is still unclear.

JUMARS—Metal climbing hardware held in the hand. Used to slide up and grip a line.

KARST—The descriptive term for eroded limestone terrain, characterized by sinkholes, depressions, blind streams, and exposed limestone ledges. Named after the classic area in Yugoslavia where this type of landscape is common.

PRUSIK—A method of climbing up a single rope by means of sliding knots, which hold three loops to the line. By alternating his weight, the climber "walks" up the rope on the loops, one on each leg and around the chest, sliding the knots alternatingly up the rope.

RESURGENCE—A spring (or reappearance) of water from the ground.

RIMSTONE POOL—A natural basin of water in a cave, formed by the deposit of calcite around its edge. Sometimes the water cascades over the lip of these calcite deposits to other rimstone pools at lower levels.

SCREE—The mass of loose rock that accumulates at the bottom of a cliff due to weathering. *See* TALUS.

SHOW CAVE—*See* COMMERCIAL CAVE.

SINKHOLE—A depression in the ground, usually in limestone country, and generally dry, but sometimes with a drainage opening at the bottom where water may escape. A sinkhole may sometimes be the collapsed roof of a cave.

SIPHON—A point where the ceiling comes down to, sometimes below, the level of the water.

SODA STRAWS—Thin stalactites that resemble soda straws.

SPELEOLOGIST—A person who does serious or professional work regarding the study of caves.

SPELUNKER—A cave enthusiast. Derived from the Roman word *spelunka,* roughly meaning "beneath the ground." In general terms, the spelunker is the sports caver and the speleologist is the scientific or professional caver.

STALACTITES—Drip-stone deposits resembling icicles, formed by the slow drip of mineral-laden water. They usually start on the ceiling and assume conical shapes.

STALAGMITES—Drip-stone deposits, the result of dripping water on a floor or wall. The mineral-laden water gives up some of its impurities, which accumulate to form mounds or spires. In limestone caves stalagmites are usually calcite, but can be mud, sand, or other material. Ordinarily, stalagmites form from calcite drippings of stalactites above.

TALUS—Identical to scree (q.v.) except that fracturing as well as weathering causes the falling rock.

TOURIST CAVE—*See* COMMERCIAL CAVE.

TRAVERSE—A difficult or tortuous route between two points of relative safety. In caves, usually associated with travel across areas of exposure such as water, deep pits, or rock ledges.

WILD CAVE—A cave in its natural state and undeveloped as contrasted with one exhibited to the public. The wild cave may or may not have been explored.

INDEX

Page references in italics refer to illustrations.

Q

R

S